Ritual, Secrecy, and Civil Society

Also from Westphalia Press
westphaliapress.org

Ritual, Secrecy, and Civil Society

Volume 4, Number 1
Spring 2016

Pierre Mollier,
Editor-in-Chief

WESTPHALIA PRESS
An imprint of Policy Studies Organization

Ritual, Secrecy, and Civil Society - Volume 4 - Number 1 - Spring 2016

Westphalia Press
An imprint of Policy Studies Organization
1527 New Hampshire Ave., NW
Washington, D.C. 20036
info@ipsonet.org

ISBN-13: 978-1-63391-626-5
ISBN-10: 1-63391-626-X

Cover design by Jeffrey Barnes:
jbarnes.design

Daniel Gutierrez-Sandoval, Executive Director
PSO and Westphalia Press

Updated material and comments on this edition
can be found at the Westphalia Press website:
www.westphaliapress.org

Ritual, Secrecy, and Civil Society
Volume 4, Number 1 • Spring 2016
©2016 Policy Studies Organization

Table of Contents

Ritual, Secrecy and Civil Society:
Issue No. 7, Spring 2016

Freemasonry: Spirituality and Symbolism

Foreword by Pierre Mollier, Editor-in-Chief

The French Revolution was an event whose consequences extended well beyond France and lasted for the whole of the nineteenth century. Our first article examines a little-known episode showing the way religion was considered during those years. The Roman Catholic Church's opposition to the new régime initially aroused strong anticlericalism, which was then followed by different attempts to create a new religion. According to the mindset of the time, a political régime had necessarily to be underpinned by religious concepts. One of these plans for a new religion was "Theophilanthropy," which was closely related to freemasonry.

French freemasonry is often difficult to understand from the British or American point of view. In France and beyond, in countries of Latin culture such as southern Europe and South America, the burden of power wielded by the Roman Catholic Church caused liberals to enter Masonic lodges in massive numbers; they then proceeded to turn these into organizations ready to combat in favor of the new ideas. André Combes, one of the most respected French Masonic historians, first offers us an overall picture of the history of French lodges from 1815 to 1945. He then introduces an author, Oswald Wirth (1860-1943), who was a very important figure in the history of Latin freemasonry. At a time when the lodges were deeply engaged in the political fight to establish democracy in France, this French Mason of Swiss origin pleaded for a restoration of work on initiation and symbolism. He was at the origin of a real "symbolic revival" which would gradually spread to all Masonic circles. A whole facet of freemasonry in Latin countries today has its origin in the writings and ideas disseminated by Oswald Wirth between 1882 and his death in 1943.

Next, we are offered a fine portrait of a man, Curuppumullage Jinarajadasa (1875-1953), who was at the crossroads between freemasonry and Theosophy; this is followed by a study of freemasonry in Turkey. Although, of course, freemasonry originated in Europe, it very quickly took root in other continents, and the encounter between freemasonry and other cultures makes for a fascinating study.

doi: 10.18278/rscs.4.1.1

Theophilanthropy: A (Masonic) Plan for Deist Worship

Pierre Mollier

Can deism be the object of worship? This was the ambition of Theophilanthropy, a movement that is largely forgotten today but which, for almost two years from 18 Fructidor year V (September 4, 1797) to 30 Prairial year VII (June 18, 1799), was practically the "official religion" of France. In the beginning, it was no more than a strange utopist project, like several others that existed during the Revolution. But the political situation and the protection of one of the strong men of the revolutionary government, the "Director" La Révellière-Lépeaux, brought it to center stage. After tracing the main paths of this curious story[1], we will investigate the principals professed by the Theophilanthropists, and then explore the numerous links with Freemasonry.

I. The Origin and History of a New Religion

In 1796, Chemin fils, a young and relatively obscure bookseller, published a plan for deist worship entitled *Manuel des Théoanthropophiles*. He was not the first but, to his great surprise, the book achieved a certain success and he found several enthusiastic readers who pressed him to move on from the plan to the organization of a small circle that would put into practice the deist worship outlined in the work.

Some of the enlightened bourgeoisie, such as the benefactor of the blind Valentin Haüy or the deputy Goupil de Prefelne, gathered with their families in the little Church of St. Catherine to celebrate the *Father of Nature* and to teach each other the purest of morals. They also slightly changed the name proposed by Chemin to "Theophilanthropists", which better suited their tastes. Then, what could have remained as an astonishing experience moved, thanks to the political situation, into the grand narrative of history. In 1797, the leaders of the Directory were faced with the slow revival of conservative and monarchist opinion in the country. The "refractory priests" were at the forefront of this opposition to the Republic. Moreover, as men of the eighteenth century, the republicans were convinced that politics and religion were intimately linked, and that revolution in the political domain must be accompanied by grand changes in the religious sphere. This opinion can be found not only among Robespierre's disciples, but also among practically all of the supporters of the Revolution, even the most moderate. Thus that Egeria of the liberals, Madame de Staël, could write:

> The system of the French Republic can only be based on the total acceptance of reason as the foundation for all institutions

---

[1] The history of Theophilanthropy has been magisterially traced by the great historian of the French Revolution, Albert Mathiez, in a landmark thesis that remains, more than a century after its publication, the essential work of reference. We rely in part on this study, which we use extensively: Albert Mathiez, *La Théophilanthropie et le culte décadaire 1796-1801, Essai sur l'histoire religieuse de la Révolution*, Paris, Félix Alcan, 1903, reprinted by Slatkine Reprints, Genève, 1975. One may also consult: Jean-Pierre Chantin, "Les adeptes de la théophilanthropie, pour une autre lecture d'Albert Mathiez", in *Rives méditerranéennes*, No. 14 (2003) Révolution et minorités religieuses, p. 63-73.

doi: 10.18278/rscs.4.1.2

and all ideas... All religion that has as its foundation what we call dogmas, which is to say mysteries, and which rest on blind faith, all religions of this type are of necessity based on the same arguments which, applied in a different context, hold up the nobility and the monarchy.[2]

Catholicism is inextricably linked to the Monarchy, and if the Republic wishes to build a durable foundation, it must rely on a religious revolution. This was the subject of a great speech made by Director La Révellière-Lépeaux at the Institute – the temple of republican thought – on 12 Floréal of Year V (1 May 1797). Heirs to the Girondins, the men of the Directory were "moderate republicans, though their republicanism was not moderate"[3]. Despite the aversion they might have felt for Robespierre and the failure of the cult of the Supreme Being, the establishment of the Republic did not seem possible to them unless accompanied by the advent of a new religion that would plant in the hearts of citizens the ideas and morals of the Republic. The picture of the religion that La Révellière deemed necessary in order to establish the moral unity of the French people coincided broadly with the new faith professed by the small group of Theophilanthropists. Thus the group was thrust into the spotlight. Montesquieu had shown that the Republic was based on virtue, and the new religion would teach that virtue to the people.

The cult of the Theophilanthropists arose in an era when a faction hostile to the Republic was threatening France with violent disturbance. Also [...] a religious

institution based on philosophical principles tended by its nature to strengthen the Republican government.[4]

As a result of the fame that La Révellière-Lépeaux's great speech had assured them, the Theophilanthropists would soon draw a whole crowd of new devotees, many of them sincere and others aware of the almost official protection granted by the government. The coup d'état of 18 Fructidor Year V (September 4, 1797) made La Révellière-Lépeaux – whose name has now fallen into obscurity – the leading figure of the regime. The political success of its protector promoted the development of the new religion in the country. In Paris, almost 18 places of Theophilanthropic worship were established in several churches, renamed appropriately: Temple of the Reunion (Saint-Merri), Temple of the Social Contract (Saint-Eustache), Temple of Fidelity (Saint-Gervais), Temple of Concord (Saint-Sulpice), etc. The chronicle of the allocation of different churches to the Theophilanthropists and the controversies that this provoked is a whole separate, and often comical, side of their history. Theophilanthropist groups were established in many provincial towns. Protected and favored by the government, the church experienced sustained growth for almost two years. For the most part, however, the fall of its defender La Révellière-Lépeaux in the coup d'état of 30 Prairial Year VII (June 18, 1799) marked the end of the adventure. To everyone's surprise, however, Theophilanthropy survived this heavy blow and, despite the suspicion it aroused due to its

---

[2] *Des circonstances actuelles qui peuvent terminer la Révolution et des principes qui doivent fonder la République en France* (1798), Editions Fischbacher, Paris, 1906, p. 220. Quoted by Mathiez, *op. cit.*, p. 267-268.
[3] This phrase apparently comes from Waldeck-Rousseau. Historians apply it to the liberal republicans of the Third Republican, which in some ways the men of the Directorate preceded. .
[4] *Qu'est-ce que la Théophilanthropie?* p. 16.

links with the ousted government, remained very active in Paris and in the provinces. It would not disappear until the Concordat of 1801, when the papal negotiators made its suppression a condition of the agreement with the First Consul.

II. Simple and Practical Principles

As he himself said in his *Manuel des Théophilanthropes* (1797), Chemin had done no more than to set down on paper the doctrine of the "natural religion". This holds to two principles, or "dogmas" in the language of the era:

> *"Theophilanthropists believe in the existence of God and in the immortality of the soul. The wonder of the universe attests to the existence of a first being. The faculty we have for thought assures us that we ourselves have a principle superior to matter which will survive the dissolution of our bodies. The existence of God and the immortality of the soul do not require long demonstrations; they are the truths of feelings that each of us has in his heart."*[5]

As truths of feelings, the two dogmas of Theophilanthropy had another essential justification in the eyes of the new church – they were useful:

Theophilanthropists hold yet more firmly to this double belief because it is as necessary to the preservation of society as to the happiness of the individual.[6]

Good is everything that tends to preserve man or perfect him. Evil is everything that tends to degrade man or deteriorate him.

There are no good acts except those which are useful.[7]

Principles are true when they are useful, but also when they are simple. The revealed religions have obscured their primitive simplicity by encumbering the principles with "theological" myths and "sacerdotal" customs. At times the Theophilanthropists thought to call themselves "primitive Christians", as they believed that they professed the original faith. This idea of a "natural religion" dominated the second part of the eighteenth century and the first two thirds of the nineteenth century. For the "philosophes", the different revealed religions all derived from this primitive religion which the priests had sadly overloaded with useless dogmas and obscure myths in order to legitimize the "priesthood". This thesis would be defended and promoted by a book – in fact ten volumes riddled with Latin – that would long resonate in men's minds: *L'Origine de tous les Cultes ou Religion Universelle* by Dupuis. The author was already a renowned intellectual at the end of the Ancien Régime, but he had to wait for the Revolution before he could publish his impious theories, and his magnum opus did not appear until 1794[8]. The Theophilanthropists wanted to rediscover and revive this "principal", by which they meant primitive and universal, religion:

There are many faiths and they may have within them infinite variations, but

---

[5] *Manuel des Théophilanthropes ou adorateurs de Dieu et amis des hommes contenant l'exposition de leurs dogmes, de leur morale et de leurs pratiques religieuses, avec une instruction sur l'organisation et la célébration du Culte*, second edition, L'Abeille, Paris, An V-1797, p. 11-12.

[6] *Manuel des Théophilanthropes...*, op. cit., p. 12.

[7] *Manuel des Théophilanthropes...*, op. cit., p. 19.

[8] *Origine de tous les Cultes ou Religion Universelle* by Dupuis, Citizen of France, in Paris, with H. Agasse, Year III of the Republic, one and indivisble.

there cannot be but one sole religion, the universal religion.[9]

With their feeling, their utility and their simplicity, the Theophilanthropists were the loyal sons of Rousseau and Voltaire. Due to the value they ascribed to simplicity and their allergy to "theological trickery" typical of eighteenth century philosophy, it is therefore quite difficult to go much further into the doctrine of the Theophilanthropists. When a Protestant society invited them to reveal the detail of their "confession of faith", Chemin replied that this would:

require a theological discussion and in consequence draw me beyond both my personal principles and those of Theophilanthropy.[10]

Moreover:

What God is, what the soul is, how God rewards the good and punishes the evil, these are questions beyond the scope of the Theophilanthropists' inquiries. They are convinced that there is too much distance between God and his creation for his creation to pretend to known Him.[11]

Finally, the "philosophical" claims of Theophilanthropy touched more on the moral and social ideas it professed than on its religious concepts. For the Theophilanthropists, the idea of God was more sentimental, literary, and poetic than truly theological. To grasp it, one should consider Voltaire's Prayer or take as one's guide Victor Hugo in the admirable tenth chapter of *Les Misérables* entitled "The

Bishop in the Presence of an Unknown Light". The good priest Bienvenu braves the condemnation of Bourbon Restoration society by going to visit in his final moments G., a former member of the National Convention. They fall into conversation and, sensing his end approaching:

The former representative of the people made no reply. He was seized with a fit of trembling. He looked towards heaven, and in his glance a tear gathered slowly. When the eyelid was full, the tear trickled down his livid cheek, and he said, almost in a stammer, quite low, and to himself, while his eyes were plunged in the depths:—

"O thou! O ideal! Thou alone existest!"

The Bishop experienced an indescribable shock.

After a pause, the old man raised a finger heavenward and said:—

"The infinite is. He is there. If the infinite had no person, person would be without limit; it would not be infinite; in other words, it would not exist. There is, then, an I. That I of the infinite is God."

But in passing from theory into practice, in experimenting with the establishment of a genuine faith, the leaders of the young Church would discover that it is not always easy to hold onto simplicity of principles. Certainly:

To adore God is above all to obey his law, which he has clearly explained to us via that internal feeling that carries us towards

---

[9] *Qu'est-ce que la Théophilanthropie? op. cit.*, p. 32.
[10] *Qu'est-ce que la Théophilanthropie? ou mémoire contenant l'origine et l'histoire de cette institution; ses rapports avec le Christianisme et l'aperçu de l'influence qu'elle peut avoir sur tous les cultes, en réponse aux questions posées par la Société Teylerienne de Harlem (en Hollande)*, 2nd edition, Paris, La Libre Conscience, 1868, p. 23.
[11] *Manuel des Théophilanthropes…, op. cit.*, p. 13.

good and turns us away from evil, and which we call our conscience.[12]

Moreover, the Theophilanthropists *"do not attach any superstitious importance to external practices"* and *"they consider their faith not as a tribute which God has need of, but as a means of moral education and fraternal reunion"*[13]. In the beginning, the organization of the faith was effectively going to be very simple:

Some moral inscriptions, a simple altar on which they lay, as a symbol of their gratitude for the Creator's blessings, some flowers or some fruits depending on the season, and a rostrum for lectures and discussion – that is all the ornamentation of their Temples.[14]

"A paterfamilias, properly and simply dressed and bare-headed, gives readings of the first two chapters from this manual about their dogmas and morality, and of a paragraph on the day-to-day conduct of the Theophilanthropists.

After this reading … [he] recites aloud the prayer Father of Nature

The attendants repeat in the same manner in low voices.

They sit to hear lectures or moral discussions which accord with the principles of … religions, of benevolence and of universal tolerance [...].

These lectures or discussions are interspersed with song.[15]

At the same time, however, the legitimate concern to make the faith

better organized and more attractive, and the necessity of highlighting – and even symbolically rewarding – some people's engagement in the life of the Church led to an enrichment of the Theophilanthropist liturgy that would cause debate. Controversy would notably form around the question of the "priesthood". For the philosophers of the eighteenth century, priests were one of the plagues on all civilizations. They had invented the idea of a priesthood in order to ensure their power over the people, while God naturally had no need of intermediaries between himself and men. A philosophical religion, as Theophilanthropy wished to be, should therefore not have priests. In the beginning, worship was led only by a "Paterfamilias", chosen almost randomly or appointed by turn, whose costume was limited to being *"properly and simply dressed and bare-headed"*. Naturally, however, the conduct of the ceremony and the choice and explanation of texts presented to the faithful required particular skills and, after several months, the Church saw the emergence of personalities who took control of the office of "Paterfamilias" and who began to be called "Readers" and "Orators". Soon after, the celebrant was assigned a particular uniform... which echoed others:

considering that all men who fulfill a serious function should have a corresponding appearance, and desiring that its readers and orators appear in garments that are always equally simple, neat and decent, it was thought that they could have, for religious and moral celebrations, a particular costume that would consist of a long habit of a single color. The color white was adopted as it was a symbol of the

[12] *Manuel des Théophilanthropes…, op. cit.*, p. 18.
[13] *Qu'est-ce que la Théophilanthropie ? op. cit.*, p. 25.
[14] *Manuel des Théophilanthropes…, op. cit.*, p. 33.
[15] *Manuel des Théophilanthropes…, op. cit.*, p. 36-37.

simplicity and purity of Theophilanthropic principles.[16]

Some months later, the clothing of the celebrants would see a further advance in sophistication and symbolism:

It is thought that, so that readers might appear in garments that are always equally simple, neat and decent, it would be good that they should have, for their public engagements, a particular costume that would consist of a sky-blue tunic, stretching from the collar down to the feet, with a pink belt and a white robe over it, open in front.[17]

At the same time, the Church's liturgy became richer, as can be seen from successive editions, as did, augmented and enriched each time by Chemin, the Theophilanthropic reference books that appeared under the titles *Manuals, Worship, Rituals, The Religious Year,* etc. As a "natural" religion, Theophilanthropy regulated its calendar according to the seasons of the cosmos and of human life. Thus it developed ceremonies to celebrate the milestones of the year (the solstices and equinoxes) with the *Festivals of Spring, of Summer, of Autumn* and of *Winter*[18] and the milestones of life (birth, adolescence, marriage, death, etc.).

Even if you want to stick to simple principles, when religious ideas are developed into a faith, the need for a symbolic apparatus arises.

III. Theophilanthropy and Freemasonry

In his thesis, Mathiez made a direct link between Theophilanthropy and Freemasonry. He even saw in Theophilanthropy *"an overt Masonry"*[19]. For him, Chemin was certainly a Mason, and he put many of the principles and practices of the lodges into his new religion. The question is complex because, in fact, Chemin was not just a Mason, but a very active Mason. However, his known masonic activity took place under the Bourbon Restoration and the July Monarchy, and there is no proof whatsoever that he had already been initiated during the Revolution. It should be remembered nonetheless that there were numerous initiations during the revolutionary period which the circumstances did not permit to be recorded in writing. The lodges waited for more peaceful times, around 1800, before returning to the keeping of records and tables. One indication, meanwhile, that suggests Chemin was not initiated in the era of Theophilanthropy is that he cannot be found either in the tables of lodges under the Empire. In fact, he does not appear until 1818 in the Lodge of Trinosophes. However, we do not know when he was initiated because his entry into the Trinosophes was an affiliation. It therefore remains possible – but in our view unlikely – that he had been accepted as a Mason at the beginning of the Revolution and that, for various reasons, he had not been active in Freemasonry under the Empire until he was affiliated to the

---

[16] [Jean-Baptiste Chemin], *Le Culte des Théophilanthropes ou adorateurs de Dieu et amis des hommes contenant leur manuel, leur catéchisme et recueil de discours, Lectures, Hymnes et Cantiques pour toutes leurs fêtes religieuses et morales*, third edition, J. Decker, Bâle, 1798, note 1, p. 9.

[17] J.B. Chemin, *Rituel des Théophilanthropes, contenant l'ordre de leurs différents exercices et le Recueil des Cantiques, Hymnes et Odes adoptés dans les différents Temples tant à Paris que des départements...* Paris, An VI (1798), note 1, p. 4.

[18] One can find the details of the "liturgical calendar" of the Theophilanthropists and the rituals and readings suggested for the different ceremonies in *Le Culte des Théophilanthropes...*, op. cit., Bâle 1778.

[19] Albert Mathiez, *op. cit.*, p. 83.

Trinosophes in 1818. In any case, whether Chemin was or was not a Mason is ultimately of secondary importance, as the principles of Freemasonry were almost in the public domain at the time, and there were certainly quite a number of Masons in the story of Theophilanthropy.

While the two principles of Theophilanthropy – the existence of God and the immortality of the soul – are drawn directly from the Deism of the Enlightenment, they also have much older traditional religious sources. In fact, these two ideas are often associated with, for example, the Noahides, those sages of Antiquity who revered the precepts given by God to Noah[20]. Anderson's Constitutions reference the Noahides in order to anchor the origins of Freemasonry. Equally, in Paris in the years preceding the Revolution, the Philalèthes of the famous Loge des Amis Réunis saw in these two principles the pinnacle of masonic ideas[21]. If at the time Chemin had had no personal contact with Freemasonry whether directly or by proxy through friends (which, it must be said, would be truly astonishing) – this man of letters could have discovered it through numerous works. Note, for example, that at the beginning of the Revolution, there appeared a pamphlet which divulged in detail the rituals of a masonic Deist system which showed numerous features shared with Theophilanthropy: The Elect of Truth. Originally, The Elect of Truth was a

system of high degrees established by the Masons of Rennes in 1770[22]. The system then won a certain amount of success and was disseminated in several towns in the west and in Paris. At the top degree of the system, the Elect of Truth professed a militant Voltarian Deism – which is to say a rational Deism extremely hostile to revealed religions. As a testimony of the time also affirms: "These notebooks were divulged and publicly sold during the revolution, and served as the basis for the religious faith that the republic has adopted"[23].

But if Freemasonry did probably play a role in the origins and the history of Theophilanthropy, it was above all in the new faith's afterlife that it would have a major presence. Somehow, once forbidden, Theophilanthropy would take refuge in the lodges. Chemin-Dupontès became a masonic luminary, and even a luminary of the Ancient and Accepted Scottish Rite. Thus he was the author, in 1823 of a memoir entitled *Mémoire sur l'Écossisme par le F∴ Chemin-Dupontès G∴. Inspecteur Général du Rit Écossais, Député au G∴ Orient de France, Vénérable de la R∴L∴. des Sept Écossais Réunis et auteur de l'Encyclopédie maçonnique.* After twenty years, he would graft into Freemasonry many of the ideas of the revolutionary religion:

The initiated, reborn into a new life, recognized that many teachers ∴, and he himself perhaps, had allowed themselves to be led by two opposing errors ... a lack

---

[20] See, for example, the article devoted to them in the *Encyclopédie* of Diderot and d'Alembert: "*Noahides.... The precepts given to this patriarch and his children seem to be no more than the precepts of the natural rights ... to adore the creator* [they must] *inspire the sentiments of humanity in all our behavior. Encyclopédie ou Dictionnaire raisonné...*, Genève, Pellet, 1778, Volume 23, p. 5.

[21] "Première Circulaire..." in: Charles Porset, *Les Philalèthes et les Convents de Paris, une politique de la folie*, Honoré Champion, Paris, 1996, p. 262-263.

[22] See: Pierre Mollier, "Un système rationaliste de Hauts-grades au XVIIIe siècle : Les Elus de la Vérité", in *Studia latomorum & historica-Mélanges offerts à Daniel Ligou*, collected by Charles Porset, Honoré Champion, 1998, p. 313-326.

[23] *Idem*, p. 324.

of faith … or a superstitious faith. He freely adopted the enlightened faith that the initiation presented him with, this simple and reasoned faith that makes him recognize his relations with his creator and with his peers … encourages him in the practice of all public and private virtues.[24]

During the Revolution, the citizens of Strasbourg had practiced the new faiths "with gravity and conviction"[25]. In 1827, an Alsacien Mason, Brother Riebesthal, published a curious pamphlet entitled *Rituel maçonnique pour tous les rites [Masonic Rituals for All Ceremonies]*[26]. It is a surprise to discover there rituals for conducting *The Festival of the Revival of Nature at the spring equinox, The Festival of the Triumph of Light at the summer solstice, The Festival of Nature's Rest at the autumn equinox,* and *The Festival of the Regeneration of Light at the winter solstice.* Nature, regeneration – the very titles of these festivals, completely unknown in eighteenth century Freemasonry, of course recall the religious experiments of the Revolution[27]. This association and the religious orientation that it suggests are confirmed in two other rituals explained by Riebesthal: the "Masonic Baptism of a Louveton (at under three years of age)", and the "Confirmation of a Louveton (who has reached the age of seventeen)". Finally, the work concludes with a list of "Common holidays during the year" which also unavoidably recalls the republican

calendar and Theophilanthropy. Each of the 52 Sundays of the year has been assigned a moral or philosophical theme as part of a Festival of Honor, of Sincerity, of Brotherly Love, of Wisdom, of Patriotism, of Candor, of Reason, of Patience, of Mercy, and of Concord. Riebesthal explains that these ceremonies are aimed at:

better experiencing the effect and feeling the advantage of the reasonable, natural and purely moral faith that Freemasonry should profess[28]. … The ceremonies that it employs and the emblems with which it adorns its temples have the goal of inspiring man with the most pure morality, of interesting him in the good of humanity, of revealing to him the truth and of making him attentive to the phenomena of nature, to lift his soul and urge him to contemplate the night sky where myriad stars in their resplendent light announce to him and prove to him the existence of the incomprehensible Being who possesses the ultimate in power, in grandeur, and in all the perfections.[29]

These words trace almost verbatim the maxims of Theophilanthropy. It should be no surprise, then, that the Paris correspondent of Brother Riebesthal and his Strasbourg Lodges was Brother Chemin-Dupontès. These para-masonic ceremonies, which were all the rage in the nineteenth century and are still sometimes practiced today – "adoption" or "masonic baptism",

---

[24] *Cours pratique de Franc-maçonnerie publié sur la demande et sous les auspices de la R ∴ L ∴ Isis-Montyon,* by F ∴ C ∴ Dupontès, third section, degree of Master, Paris, 1841, p. 182.

[25] Albert Mathiez, *op. cit.,* p. 491-492.

[26] Ch.-G. Riebesthal, *Rituel maçonnique pour tous les rites,* Strasbourg, Silbermann, s.d. [1826].

[27] See: Pierre Mollier, "Chrétien-Guillaume Riebesthal: Des religions de la Révolution aux cérémonies paramaçonniques " in *Les Frères Réunis à Strasbourg, une loge maçonnique engagée,* catalog of the exhibition presented at the History Museum of the City of Strasbourg from October 15, 2011 to February 5, 2012, ID Edition, 2011, pp. 43-47.

[28] Ch.-G. Riebestal, *op. cit.,* p. 8.

[29] Ch.-G. Riebestal, *op. cit.,* Preface, p. VIII.

"conjugal recognition" or "masonic marriage", "funereal handling" or "masonic obsequies" – are in origin directly descended from Theophilanthropy. From the aftermath of the Revolution and up until 1877, the Grand Orient de France considered Freemasonry as the incarnation of natural religion, and considered itself a deist church. In some cases, consciously and for the most part unconsciously, it presented itself as the continuation of Theophilanthropy. And 1877 did not mark, as it is sometimes suggested, a break with traditional Judeo-Christian Freemasonry, but a handover from the older generation professing the rational deism of Voltaire and the Revolution, to the new generation of the 1860s, who were disciples of the rational agnosticism of Auguste Comte.

Theophilanthropy had wanted to be a religion reduced to the essential principles of the religious. Freemasonry of the nineteenth century was profoundly marked by the religious heritage of the Revolution, and for many it certainly was – at that time at least – a religion reduced to principles.

The last of the Theophilanthropists were still trying to gather for their worship on 20 Vendémiaire Year X (October 12, 1801). By order of the government, they were forbidden access to their temples and asked to disperse. After some protestation and vain attempts at approaching the First Consul, who had at one time been quite closely linked to La Revellière-Lépeaux, the purest cult of the natural religion was buried in obscurity. The Theophilanthropists preached tolerance. They proclaimed from the pulpit – professing this religion on which all men could agree – that they were friends to all faiths. They were nonetheless considered, by deeply Catholic France, as the religious arm of the Revolution and the

enemy to be defeated. The historic episode of Theophilanthropy may seem picturesque and anecdotal, but it nonetheless reveals structural elements of the religious and political history of our country. While in Great Britain and the Anglo-Saxon world, deism fits into the continuity of Christianity and appears as a prolonged Unitarianism, in France both in the domain of ideas and in the domain of history, deism is a break with Christianity and clearly fits into the critical camp of rationalism and the Enlightenment. It is probably this philosophical and religious context that explains in part the evolution of Freemasonry in the final third of the nineteenth century.

Appendix 1

Voltaire's Prayer[30]

So it is no longer to men that I address myself, it is to you, God of all beings, of all worlds and of all times. If it is permitted for weak creatures lost in the vastness and imperceptible to the rest of the universe to dare to demand anything of you, you who have given everything, you whose decrees are as immutable as they are eternal, then deign to look with pity on the mistakes attached to our nature, and do not let these mistakes become our calamities. You have not given us a heart to hate ourselves, or hands to kill ourselves. Make it so that we mutually aid each other to bear the burden of a painful and transitory life; that the small differences in the clothes which cover our foolish bodies, in all our inadequate languages, in all our ridiculous customs, in all our imperfect laws, in all our senseless opinions, in all our conditions so disproportionate in our eyes, and so equal before you; that all these little nuances that

---

[30] Voltaire, *Traité sur la tolérance à l'occasion de la mort de Jean Calas* (1763), extract from Chapter XXIII.

distinguish these atoms known as men be not the signals for hate and for persecution; that those who light candles in broad daylight to worship you tolerate those who are content with the light of your sun; that those who cover their dress in white cloth to show that we must love you not hate those who say the same thing under a coat of black wool; that it be the same to adore you in a dialect formed from an ancient language or in a dialect more modern; that those whose dress is colored red or purple, and who rule over a little parcel of a little heap of the mud of this world, and who possess a few round pieces of a certain metal, enjoy without pride that which they call grandeur and wealth, and that the others watch them without envy, for you know that in these vanities there is nothing to envy, nor to be proud of.

Let all men remember that they are brothers! Let them hold in horror tyranny exercised over souls, as they hold in contempt the banditry that seizes by force the fruits of peaceful labor and industry! If the scourges of war are inevitable, let us not hate one another in the bosom of peace, and let us use the brief moment of our existence to praise in a thousand different languages, from Siam to California, your kindness which has given us this moment.

that you have established in your wisdom and that you maintain with your providence, and I submit myself forever to this universal order.

I do not ask you for the power to do good. For you have given me this power and, along with it, conscience to love good, reason to understand it, and liberty to choose it. I would not then have any excuse if I were to do evil. I make before you the commitment to use my freedom only in order to do good, no matter what attractions evil might seem to offer.

I will never address indiscreet prayers to you. You know the creatures that have come from your hand, their needs no more escape your eyes than do their most secret thoughts. I pray only that you redress the mistakes of the world and my own mistakes, for almost all the evils that afflict men come from their mistakes.

Full of confidence in your justice and in your kindness, I resign myself to whatever comes, my sole wish being that your will be done.

Appendix 2

The invocation of the Father of Nature is the principal prayer of the Theophilanthropists [31]:

Father of nature, I bless your kindnesses and I thank you for your gifts.

I admire the beautiful order of things

---

[31] *Manuel des Théophilanthropes…, op. cit.*, pp. 29-31.

Freemasonry Within French Society Between 1815 and 1945

André Combes

This paper will look at "Freemasonry within French Society between 1815 and 1945", not simply at the Grand Orient de France. There may indeed have been the odd spot of trouble on occasion between the two main branches of Freemasonry in France – the Grand Orient de France (GODF) on the one hand, which was associated with the French Rite, and the group that, in 1894, would assume the title of Grande Loge de France (GLDF) on the other, which observed a Scottish Rite. But, despite this trouble, in reality there was no difference between them in terms of their recruitment nor their values, and both battled equally during the Third Republic to ensure the Republic was (in the expression of the day) *"democratic, social and universal"*. Both endured the same attacks and the same repression meted out by the Vichy regime and Nazi occupying forces, and members from both organizations participated jointly in the French Resistance. It would therefore be hard to distinguish the way that Masonry was viewed by Frédéric Desmons or Charles Debierre, who ran GODF, from the way that it was viewed by Gustave Mesureur or General Peigné, in charge of GLDF. In the years leading up to the Second World War, Pierre Brossolette belonged to both organizations and people like Marc Rucart, who would go on to represent the Masons unofficially at the Conseil national de la Résistance (National Council of the Resistance), or Pierre Bloch, who would become president of the International League against Anti-Semitism, also belonged to another Lodge, the Loge du Droit Humain.

If we are to locate the Masons within French society, we must first and foremost assess their numbers and see where they fitted in the social hierarchy. Freemasonry, by its very foundations, had never been a mass association, but it had always been firmly rooted within the fabric of society. However, out in the provinces, there were whole areas that the Masons had left for years totally devoid of Freemasonry, and not all of the states across France were covered by the various Lodges – something that would limit the potential influence of Freemasonry. The numbers of active Masons can be estimated to have been in the region of 12,000 in 1830, 15,000 in 1848, and 24,000 in 1870, with a large degree of flux that would have been due, in part, to the precarious living conditions. After 1870, the Masonic organizations started to keep files, so from then on we are able to be more precise. By the end of the century, GODF still only had a mere 18,000 members but, by 1910, the figure had risen to more than 31,000. And membership of GLDF, which had stood at no more than a few thousand when the organization began, had already reached 8,000. These rises can be attributed to the militant fervor of the Brethren at the time of the *Bloc des Gauches* (a coalition of republican parties active during the Third Republic). Come 1939, there were 43,000 men and fewer than 2,000 women in the Masons. And numbers then fell sharply when the War came to an end, dipping to about 15,000 for the three main organizations.

Women would remain excluded from the Masons until 1893 when a new Lodge was formed (the Loge du Droit Humain)

doi: 10.18278/rscs.4.1.3

with a feminist vocation. Rural populations continued to be under-represented, except in regions where the influence of Christianity had faded, and given also the fact that the temples were all located in the towns. Changes in the pattern of recruitment began to be seen in the first half of the nineteenth century when a significant percentage of shopkeepers and manual workers – artisans, foremen as well as laborers, some tradesmen too of different kinds – began to join the Masons, alongside all the notaries, lawyers, traders, businessmen, people of private means, landowners, and merchants, from the lower and middle ranks of the bourgeoisie. Some Lodges started to run evening classes, providing either general learning or more specific vocational training for their members, some of whom were practically illiterate, and also for non-Masons too. This is another thing that accounts for the growing interest amongst the Masons, from 1830 onwards, in questions of health, morality and education for the masses. And it also accounts for the significant sums contributed by the Masons towards philanthropic causes such as asylums, charitable work to help children, or the distribution of soup, bread tokens or meat. Under the Third Republic, in addition to the Masonic orphanage, the Masons would continue to provide a network of local job centers, a welfare society for people injured at work and free lessons for the public given by GODF after the war of 1870.

Freemasonry may have appealed to people from the working classes who were self-educated, but it was rarely of interest to those workers, often of peasant stock, employed in big industry – despite the funds made available for that purpose by the different Masonic groups. From 1870 onwards, to join the Masons became more a matter of political choice, a statement of anti-clerical, republican sympathies.

As Freemasonry started to become more intellectually demanding, it was civil servants and white-collar workers who tended to be more heavily represented. Growth, in particular, in the number of primary school teachers joining the Masons led to an increase in the size of some provincial Lodges by as much as a third in the 1900s. And, after the police began to support the republican cause, police officers – a group previously suspected of spying on the Masons – came to be well represented. The presence of the military within the Masons varied considerably accordingly to the period. During the July Monarchy, numbers were quite sizeable, particularly in Algeria – so much so that Marshal Soult would attempt to ban his officers from attending a Lodge for fear they would become contaminated there by republican ideas. Later, however, the numbers fell due to the level of mistrust, if not open hostility, that soldiers on the republican wing had to endure from their pro-Church, and often pro-Monarchy, staff headquarters – something that, come 1904, would be one of the causes of the *affaire des Fiches* (when it was discovered that information on people's religious affiliations was being collected and used to determine promotions).

Freemasonry was essentially under attack, especially after 1815. The excommunication order issued back in 1738 applied after the Concordat (between Napoleon and the Pope) and later, with the return of the Bourbons and a period of "White Terror", anti-Masonic feeling of Catholic origin would come to be fostered through the writings of Abbé Barruel or his imitators, in which the Masons were portrayed as being responsible for the crimes of the French Revolution, or even as satanical. The number of conservative Catholics represented in the Lodges grew smaller and smaller. They were replaced by activists of one sort or another, religious minorities (Protestants, Jews, progressive Muslims, notably from the Ottoman Empire), deists in the mold of Voltaire or Rousseau, and later, atheists – by those parts of French society inspired by the Enlightenment, liberal, then democrat, even socialist. Hence we find by 1849 that, even if GODF was still basing itself on a belief in God (without greater specificity) and immortality of the soul, it now liked to see itself as a philosophical and progressive organization too and adopted the motto "liberty, equality and fraternity" – a motto that it mistakenly believed to be Masonic in origin.

The second wave of opposition to Freemasonry came later. The Masons were already being vilified by the pro-Catholic, pro-Monarchy right, standing accused of wanting to turn France into a non-Christian country and promoting a secular education system through the Ferry laws. Then, when passions were running high at the time of the Dreyfus affair and the Masons came out in 1898 in favor of reviewing the court's decision, they were accused by nationalists and anti-semites of "cosmopolitanism" and "anti-patriotism". These battles would leave their mark, to the point where eventually, in 1935, republicans on the center-right like Tardieu and René Coty would vote in favor of a ban on Freemasonry (which was being falsely portrayed at the time by Xavier Vallat and other leading lights on the extreme-right as a secret society).

The poor may, during the French Revolution, have demanded that there should be only one Lodge in the future: the Lodge of the People. Even so, there would be no hostility towards the Masons amongst those on the far left. Many socialists and, after Proudhon, even some anarchists and radical trade unionists would join the ranks of the Masons. Later on, though, a socialist movement grew up around Mussolini in Italy that was positively anti-Mason and another, around Jules Guesde in France, that was suspicious of Freemasonry, all in the name of class struggle. The Third Congress of the Communist International held in Moscow in 1922 imposed a ban on belonging to both the Masons and the Communist International, as it did on belonging to the Human Rights League too – an organization that had been established during the Dreyfus affair and counted many Masons amongst its members. But there were few defections in reality. The most painful one was the defection of André Marty, who had spearheaded the Black Sea mutiny and was then a member of GLDF (and would later go on to lead the French Communist Party). And let's not forget that this ostracism would cease in 1945 when everyone joined forces to fight the Nazis.

Public suspicion of a closed society from which people felt themselves excluded was understandable, despite the efforts made by the Lodges to open themselves up, in particular through conferences, brochures, public banquets, open meetings and newspaper articles. Nonetheless, because of their work for the under-privileged, the Masons did enjoy a certain popularity and, in republican circles, they continued to be well-liked. The most obvious example of popular support was the large crowd that turned out to cheer the Masonic procession that marched from the Hôtel de Ville in Paris to the city's ramparts on April 29, 1871, calling on the Versailles government to open up negotiations with the Paris Commune so as to bring to a conclusion the terrible civil war being waged under the gaze of the Prussians. The Brethren fought bravely on the barricades, with all their regalia, in the firm belief that their Masonic principles compelled them to take the revolutionary path.

In the early part of the history of the Masons between 1815 and 1865, the separate branches of Freemasonry in France had need of protectors such as the Duke of Decazes in 1815. GODF, in particular, had been forced to submit to the iron rule of the Prince of Murat during the period from the coup d'état of December 2, 1851 through to 1860. The Lodges were kept under surveillance and had to avoid any subversive political discussion or criticism of religions during the course of their meetings, in the vicinity of the temple and during their meals. But all you had to do in fact was speak up for Voltaire or condemn fanaticism and superstition, and it would have been understood which Church you were alluding to. If you spoke out in praise of liberty and equality in 1835 at a time when you were forbidden from calling yourself a republican, it would have been quite clear to your contemporaries what you really meant. Freemasons in nineteenth-century France saw themselves not only as heirs to the ancient mysteries and the master-builders but also, and especially, as heirs to the Enlightenment and the Revolution – first, the Revolution of 1789, the revolution of fundamental human rights and abolition of privilege, and then the Revolution of 1793, this time in the name of their republican ideals.

During the Restoration, few of the other Lodges took much interest in the coup d'état that Les Amis de la Vérité sought to incite (Les Amis de la Vérité was a Lodge born out of the secret society known as *La Charbonnerie*, with close ties to the Italian *Carbonari*). However, at the end of Charles X's reactionary reign, the hostility felt by Masons towards the Bourbon family finally showed itself in the Masonic march that was organized in 1829 for the arrival of Lafayette, head of the opposition, in the city of Lyon. The procession by Les Amis de la Vérité, at the time of the *Trois Glorieuses*

(the July Revolution of 1830) in memory of the four sergeants of La Rochelle was the first public demonstration by Masons in favor of the Republic, at a time when most Masons still believed that Louis-Philippe, the "Citizen King", would lead the country to democracy. In 1848, with the establishment of the Republic and the first wave of reforms since the Restoration – including freedom of assembly, freedom of association, and the abolition of slavery in the colonies, a reform for which the Masons had led the campaign – Masons might have been forgiven for believing there would be a permanent march towards progress, eradication of poverty, and universal brotherhood. These illusions would, however, soon be shattered by the June workers' uprising, the French appeal in Rome for re-establishment of the Pope's authority, the (pro-Catholic) Falloux education law and then by the coup d'état of December 2, 1851.

Following the dark years of the authoritarian (Second) Empire, condemned as an alliance between Church and Army, the liberalization that occurred from 1865 onwards heralded a new era in the history of Freemasonry in France. The Lodges had more freedom to discuss any subject they pleased, even the very boldest, such as "free union" between couples, the foundations of a morality independent of religion, the different forms of socialism, the creation of co-operatives and mutual societies, and the need for school to become free of charge, compulsory and, rather late in the day in 1870, secular also, at least with respect to state education. The Lodges opened public libraries and financed free, secular-based schools. The republican victory at the polls in 1877 and the strengthening of the Republic in 1881 were also, in part, the work of the Masons, who were very active in the press and in all the local committees and organizations such as La Ligue de l'Enseignement (the League for Education). The initiation of Jules Ferry and Emile Littré into the Fraternity in the presence of Gambetta and Louis Blanc symbolized this brief union of republicans of all kinds against the monarchists. Freemasonry was therefore one of the vectors for the spread of republican ideology. It helped affection for the Republic to grow in the towns and villages of France, as well as in the colonies.

Amongst the early achievements of the republicans in office, some were more specifically due to the actions of the Masons – the Ferry laws, of course, but also the establishment of local education authorities with Charles Floquet, and the legalization of divorce and cremation. In 1887, there was the whole saga of *boulangisme*. After a bit of procrastination, the handful of Masons involved in the leadership of the Boulanger movement were sanctioned for having put the Republic in danger by allying themselves with the monarchists. This was the first example of Brethren being excluded from the Fraternity for reasons of political misconduct. Later, those who demonstrated their republican commitment would be allowed back in.

Promoting the separation of church and state was another thing that cemented the various branches of Freemasonry. Following Pastor Dide's report, the GODF convention of 1886 took up the fight for abolition of state funding for religions and separation of church and state, and the Masons became the driving force within every single anti-clerical association – particularly the free-thinker ones, which tended to be very active amongst ordinary working people. From now on, republicanism and a belief in the separation of church and state would form part of the DNA of an organization that was in effect now a secular one, where reference to GAOTU (the Grand Architect of the Universe) had become a matter of choice

and rarely preserved, or else where GAOTU was defined simply as a "creation principle" – Oswald Wirth would say a symbol – beyond all theological definition.

From the 1890s, the conventions began to be more exercised by political, social and societal issues, rather than issues internal to Freemasonry itself. The number and type of issues studied by the Lodges and reported on, along with a plethora of vows, over the course of conventions that would last an entire week was quite astonishing. The same themes were debated and analyzed in ever greater depth over a period of several years. We will confine ourselves here to a single example from the two main branches of Freemasonry. In 1896, the GODF convention discussed three socio-economic issues: introduction of a universal, progressive tax on income, establishment of a national social security and pensions fund and establishment of a Ministry of Labor with the aim of putting in place an employment code that Arthur Groussier was to oversee. The convention also dealt – this time more succinctly due to a lack of time – with the privilege of the Bank of France, weekly rest-days, provision of free local job centers to help people find work, and representation for the workers on employer management boards.

In 1913, GLDF mostly debated the arguments in favor of secular schools, the high cost of living, the Franco-German rapprochement, and the status of civil servants. Both branches celebrated the work of the cabinet led by Emile Combes, and in 1906 the GLDF convention even invited the government to draw inspiration from its example *"in order to bring in the economic and social reforms that it had promised to the electorate and the working classes"*. Among the many, many social and societal issues tackled in the years between 1890 and 1914, let us cite abolition of the death penalty, divorce by mutual consent, the plight of native women in Algeria, the plight of unmarried mothers, maternity leave, apprenticeships, the plight of farm workers, affordable housing, access to information about your paternity, the fight against syphilis and alcoholism, international arbitration and peace between nations.

All of these debates took place alongside or in advance of debates in the French Parliament. The Masons liked to elect as their leaders people who had been elected as leaders of the nation, so they could influence legislation more effectively. A large number of Masons, especially Worshipful Masters, were experienced politicians too, devoted to helping their fellow citizens, often mayors of their local community or key figures in republican associations, as can be seen from Lodge records. Even if there was only one French president, Félix Faure, who was an active Mason, there was not a single government throughout the period from 1880 to 1914 without at least some Masons in it – and this includes the government formed by the ex-Mason, Méline, which the convention accused all the same of colluding with the right. Those politicians who were also Masons, essentially radicals or socialists, were only ever rarely troubled by matters of conscience since their personal convictions were completely aligned with their Masonic promises.

However, the Masons (who took great care to stay on the fringes of electoral campaigns so they could remain embedded deep within the republican party) were not the only group of thinkers and reformers. Moreover, of the politicians who were Masons – their number must have been somewhere in the region of a quarter to a third of all deputies, given there were none on the right and very few in the center – not all were exemplary figures, or at least there were some who paid heed above all to the wishes

of their electorate. It is to be noted in this regard that the Léon Bourgeois cabinet, the only one to contain a majority of Masons, was unable to get income tax legislation passed and, particularly on questions of church and state or social questions, politicians who were Masons would often not follow the wishes of the convention, for opportunistic or financial reasons. Moreover, the Masons may have called for the separation of church and state, but they had not produced any draft legislation to that effect. So the role played by the Masons should not be under-estimated or caricatured as being solely anti-clerical, nor at the same time should it be over-estimated, as some Masons, and their enemies, have sometimes done – though, in the case of their enemies, it was in order to fight Freemasonry more effectively. The years when the role of Freemasonry was at its most influential came at the turn of the century, with the birth of the Radical and Radical-Socialist Party in 1901 (despite its name a liberal social democrat party). The Party adopted a program of reforms close to the vows made by the conventions and, with the exception of Caillaux, Goblet, and Herriot, all of the early leaders of the Party had *"hewed the rough ashlar".* The following year brought electoral success for the *Bloc des Gauches* coalition, which would proceed to enact legislation providing for the separation of church and state. Many socialists were also Masons, including (amongst other thinkers and leaders) Benoît Malon, Eugène Fournière, Jean Allemane, Jean-Baptiste Clément, and Marcel Sembat.

The Masons, like all French people, fulfilled their duties as citizens in 1914. Then, between the Wars, after the failure of the social, anti-clerical policies of the left-wing *Cartel des Gauches* in 1924, Freemasonry took a step back from politics and society, establishing a clearer distinction between the Temple on the one hand, where you reflect, and the Forum on the other, where you discuss. The burgeoning of political parties that set their own political manifestos reduced the attraction of recruiting their leaders into the Masons, and Freemasonry began to focus more on its own nature and on personal improvement for the individual, especially through initiation, cultural or philosophical work. The dictatorships in Russia, Italy, Germany, Portugal, and Spain banned Freemasonry and persecuted its members. This then served as an example to the far-right group, *Action française*, and other seditious groups, which proceeded to unleash themselves on Judeo-Masonry, weakening an institution keen to rise above it all and therefore lacking in fighting spirit and clear-sightedness. The pacifist ideas prevalent at the time, confidence in the League of Nations which the Masons had helped to found, along with Léon Bourgeois, and which they hoped to be able to make more democratic, their natural optimism, their faith in the progress of humanity – all this prevented them from paying sufficient heed to the storm-clouds gathering on the horizon. It wasn't until 1935 that GODF would adopt a strong anti-Fascist agenda with proposals for reform taken up by the left-wing Popular Front alliance. The action taken by the Masons that was most worthy of praise was the brotherly assistance that was given in 1939 to exiled Spanish republicans. That same year, I was able to put a figure on the number of Masons in the Chamber of Deputies: a third of all socialist deputies, some sixty of them, were active Masons, together with about thirty radicals out of a total of 112, including, amongst the best ones, Jean Zay and Pierre Mendèz-France. In the Senate, there were only forty or so Brethren, most of them radicals.

During the Second World War, in addition to the rounding-up of scores of Masons dismissed from the civil service or sought either for political or racial reasons, and in addition to the help given by Masons to the families of people imprisoned or deported, there was also the part played by the Masons in the French Resistance and in the colonies. The latter occurred especially in North Africa before the Anglo-American landing there, in the West Indies, and in Indochina; and then there was the Freemason, Félix Eboué, who brought Chad into de Gaulle's Free France. Two of the Resistance movements had a particularly strong Masonic presence – *Patriam Recuperare* which, in conjunction with the Lodges secretly reconstituted in the provinces, rallied round General de Gaulle and Le Coq Enchaîné, based over in Lyon. But men and women Masons, collectively or individually, were active in all the Resistance movements, in most of the underground networks, especially the professional ones (postal-workers, teachers, railway-workers...), in the infiltration of public services and in the formation of underground resistance cells. There were a high number of deaths, around 800 victims according to figures to date. Freemasonry continued to operate in the shadows and new Lodges were established, including one in the Buchenwald concentration camp.

In 1945, reduced in number but with their convictions strengthened by the battle waged against the enemy, the Masons stood ready as ever at the service of a Republic they hoped to exemplify. They had recovered their temples at least – confiscated previously by the Vichy regime – albeit standing in a terrible state, and had taken up their tools once again to continue working tirelessly for the advent of a more just and enlightened society.

Oswald Wirth and the Symbolic Revival in Freemasonry

André Combes

Oswald Wirth was born on August 5, 1860 in Brienz, in German-speaking Switzerland, near Bern. His father was an agnostic republican of protestant origin. Sentenced to nine months in prison in France for taking part in the republican and anti-clerical demonstration of June 13, 1849, he left for Brienz in Switzerland, where he worked as a successful painter. His mother was a fervent Catholic. His father, an officer in the Zouaves light infantry regiment, died at the start of the 1914 war, and his sister, Fernande, was with him in his old age. At eight years old, he became a pupil at a small seminary owned by the Benedictines. At 16, he continued his studies at the Catholic College of Fribourg, but he was expelled for being argumentative and insubordinate.

In 1879, at the age of 19, Oswald Wirth was working in London as a commercial accountant, but had little enthusiasm for this work. He cultivated his talents for magnetic healing and drawing, and took an interest in theosophy and occultism. He discovered Masonry through the brochures of Jean-Paul Mazaroz, a disciple of Fourier. Mazaroz was a sculptor and cabinet maker who had become an industrialist, and a representative of a Masonic worker sensibility open to all scientific or pseudo-scientific ideas. This sensibility was quite widespread during the Second Empire. Among other subjects, he wrote about magnetic healing.

Wirth was curious to know more about Masonry. In London, he got in touch with Joseph Silbermann, a member of the highly bourgeois *Henry IV* Lodge. Silbermann was a physicist, before becoming a laboratory assistant, then a professor at the

Collège de France. Wirth asked him about Masonry: Was it political? His answer was cryptic: "It wants to be figured out. If you are curious about its mysteries, ask to be admitted."

The Young Mason and the Ritual's Reform

With Silbermann's recommendation, although he had joined the 106th infantry regiment in Châlons-sur-Marne, he was received by the Worshipful Master of the *Bienfaisance Châlonnaise* Lodge under the *Grand Orient de France* (GODF), who presented Masonry to him as an essentially philanthropic association. He was initiated on January 28, 1884, became a Fellow on January 21, 1885 and a Master on June 9, 1885. In a provincial Lodge where the atmosphere became even more fraternal because, according to Wirth, Masonry was ill-regarded in the area, the young magnetic healer was a valued new member. He said that he met a former self-taught cook there, who was an occultism enthusiast. This is not surprising: throughout history, Lodge members have included Masons interested in all forms of esoteric studies.

The GODF's Council of the Order, having completed a revision of the Constitution and General Regulations, decided to update the rituals from when Prince Murat was Grand Master. The *Grand Collège des Rites* (GCDR: Grand College of the Rites), which acted as Supreme Council, was dissolved by the 1885 Convent, because of the absenteeism of the majority of its members. The real goal was to bring in a

doi: 10.18278/rscs.4.1.4

new, up-to-date generation of Councilors of the Order, mostly initiated under the Liberal Empire.

As arranged, this new GCDR, installed on January 6, 1886, asked the Council for its authorization to consult the Lodges about a general revision of the rituals of Symbolic Lodges. On February 13, the Council invited them to formulate their observations about their current rituals, and to propose reforms.

In Châlons, the young Wirth, elected early on as Secretary of the Lodge and who showed his dedication by visiting neighborhood Lodges, was put in charge of writing the report. The text was signed by the dynamic new Worshipful Master Maurice Bloch (a coal merchant) and by Wirth, and was very well written like all his writings to follow. It showed that perhaps even before he was admitted, he already had his views on what Masonry should be, and he tackled themes which he would develop in later years. He had a talent for persuasion, convincing the *Bienfaisance Châlonnaise* that his report should be distributed in all the Lodges.

He emphasized that in 1877, the GODF had abolished the dogmatic affirmation of the belief in God and the immortality of the soul, based on the principle of absolute freedom of conscience, that this innovation had only been introduced in 1849, and that it had therefore "returned to the true principles of the Order." He regretted only that the change had been based on the vote "which deserves only praise" to get rid of the formula ALGDGADLU (À la Gloire du Grand Architecte de l'Univers: In the Name of the Great Architect of the Universe), which Obediences put at the top of their official boards. He also emphasized that many former Brothers had left Masonry at this point, or joined another Obedience (the *Suprême Conseil de France*: Supreme Council of France, or SCDF), and that this move had caused the break with the United Grand Lodge of England (UGLE). In this first comment, he pretended to believe that it was abandoning this formula which caused the break. This was untrue and could have suggested that reintroducing it would allow the GODF to be recognized once again. Wirth was already showing his hostility to any theological affirmation, and he shifted the concept of the GAOTU from theology to symbolism. In fact, very few people left the GODF after this show of hands without a counting of votes.

This event taught him caution and made him aware of the need "to only adopt a reform when it has rigorously been proven useful," especially for anything concerning Masonic symbolism, "the unity of which constitutes the universality of our Institution." He added that:

In principle, only a Universal Masonic Congress has the right to modify this foundation of Freemasonry. It is entirely natural that if one rite is distorted, the others should refuse to recognize that rite. This is what happened to the GODF when it abolished the symbol of the GAOTU.

This suspension is the consequence of a misunderstanding, a confusion between two things, which differ as deeply as a dogma and a symbol. Dogma encourages intolerance, a sect mindset which should be resisted, but the symbol is open to interpretation by each individual, it is the very essence of our institution and gives it its reason to exist. It should therefore be carefully protected. Let us not forget that without symbolism, we could easily be just another very useful and highly estimable philanthropic society, but we would not be Freemasonry.

Symbolism is a way of thinking, it contains a whole philosophy known to the initiate, and thus gives meaning to all our rites, down to their finest details. It forms such a connected and coordinated whole that it is impossible to touch one of its parts without gradually bringing about the destruction of the whole. Consequently, symbolism can no longer go on in its current state of mutilation, and French Masonry today must choose between two things: the radical abandonment of all symbolic forms, or the regeneration of modern Masonry via the reestablishment of true initiation.

He therefore invited people to return to the overly neglected study of Masonic symbolism, which had been abandoned, meaning that there were still many Masons in Masonry, but that there were no longer any initiates.

He thought that religious cults and Masonry had drawn upon the same source: the Ancient mysteries. He said that sects had made symbolism "an instrument of domination by spreading superstition…" and asked whether Masons would have "the wisdom to return symbolism to its true destination, by using it to emancipate people and propagate true enlightenment." He continued:

What is certain is that our often bizarre ceremonies become supremely ridiculous if nobody understands their meaning, because all their merit lies in the thought behind them [...]. Let us now encourage the novice to read this mysterious book, where he will find sublime truths whose significance will be proportionate to his level of intelligence. Masonic initiation will thus become something real, and the new initiate will no longer be painfully disillusioned upon realizing that Masonic enlightenment is nothing but passwords, signs of recognition, etc.

This gave rise to a whole program: the return to the symbol of the GAOTU, very simple physical tests (he was willing to change the rituals, but to suit his ends, and this is what he did), the degree of Master being awarded only to "Masons whose character has been very seriously tested [...] with exams to obtain each Degree." This was a revolution, because at the time, there was no Masonic training: the three Degrees were generally obtained in six months, without any particular work towards salary increases.[1]

The main points of all of Wirth's future battles, at least in the GODF, GLSE (*Grande Loge symbolique ecossaise*: Scottish Grand Symbolic Lodge), and in its early days the GLDF (*Grande loge de France*: Grand Lodge of France), are already condensed within this document. In it, he is hostile to the revealed religions, adopts no position on the existence of God, refuses the intrusion of theology in Masonry and assigns it the function of studying symbolism, with the symbol of the GAOTU as its foundation, and the emancipation of peoples and the propagation of true enlightenment as its goal. He asserts that it must be based on its symbolism, revised according to ancient mysteries. He would later be more cautious about these mysteries, taking into account the builder heritage, and would direct his areas of research, "which include esotericism" towards the connections between Masonic symbolism and the symbolism of alchemy, numerology, and hermeticism.

Moreover, he was already concerned about international Masonic unity. As he was a Germanist, and his Masonic ideas were well received in Germany, he would spearhead the rapprochement between the German Obediences and the GLDF, and then in certain cases, the GODF.

---

[1] The *Rapport sur la révision des Cahiers des grades symboliques* ("Report on the Revision of the Books of Symbolic Degrees") can be found in the archives of the GODF.

Wirth's second text on Masonic symbolism was published on April 8, 1887 in Charles Fauvety's review *La Religion Laïque*. Fauvety was one of the key people in the GODF during the Second Empire. He was a deist and a spiritualist, the kind of "spiritual vagabond" that Wirth liked. The secular religion was an attempt to build a religion without dogma or clergy, but not without Freemasons. It had (very beautiful) prayers to the Supreme Being, written by Fauvety, as well as celebrations and ceremonies for the different stages of life.[2]

At the 1886 GODF Convent, the reporter indicated that 71 Lodges had answered the question on rituals (a quarter of Lodges), that six were against any change, five were for moderate reform, and 60 wanted quite major reform. *La Bienfaisance Châlonnaise* is cited as one of the three Lodges that printed their reports. The reporter concludes that the Masons are for maintaining symbolism, as a means of recognition (which is restrictive to say the least), but with clearer and more sober formulations, and without elevation above human things. The GCDR, recognized as competent concerning symbolism, was made responsible for drafting, with each Lodge free to keep its old practices.

In January 1886, it adopted the project elaborated by a commission of 12 members (including six members from the GCDR) under Louis Amiable,[3] after consulting the various suggestions, rituals from the two Scottish Obediences and even the works of Ragon, Chemin-Dupontès and others. In his conclusions, Amiable explains that the rituals abused the "noble genre," and that nobody could be exempt from the tests that the rituals prescribed for the Degrees. The project was submitted in January 1887.

But let us return to Wirth. Upon leaving military service in 1886, he moved to Paris. He became secretary to Stanislas de Guaita, who in 1888 founded the Kabbalistic order of the Rose-Croix, of which Wirth became a member. His convictions about the need for Masonry to return to its roots (at least as he imagined them) could only be strengthened by the words of his mentor, who saw the Royal Art as nothing but a dead tree. Guaita was impressed by Wirth's first works on symbolism, and wrote that they restored "Ariadne's thread," which the Masons had lost.

On March 1, 1887, Wirth joined the *Amis Triomphants* Lodge (GODF), led by Brother Vidau. When he was admitted as a member, he gave a first speech on the situation of Masonry in France, with a study on symbolism, its partisans and its adversaries. This study was later published in *La Chaîne d'Union*, a journal by Esprit-Eugène Hubert, who was a member of the dissolved GCDR, and was therefore resentful towards Amiable and his consorts. He had refused the honorary title and always been in favor of maintaining the GAOTU. However, he was not a conformist, because he had strongly contested Prince Murat.

---

[2] In December 1888, he wrote an article in the review *Le Lotus*: "La Franc-Maçonnerie au point de vue de l'Initiation occulte" ("Freemasonry from the Point of View of Occult Initiation") and in 1891, in the reviews *L'Initiation* and *L'Union occulte française*, he published "L'Initiation maçonnique" ("Masonic Initiation"); in *La Vérité philosophique* he published "Qu'est-ce qu'un Franc-Maçon ?" ("What is a Freemason") and "La Franc-Maçonnerie et la tactique anticléricale" (Freemasonry and Anticlerical Tactics".)

[3] Louis Amiable (1837–1897), lawyer, court of appeal counsel, and author of the monograph of the *Neuf Sœurs* Lodge.

Wirth's speech began:

Taking my place amid the columns of this respectable Lodge which has just honored me with membership, I feel the need to tell my new fellows in work my ideas about our institution, especially focusing on the current situation of French Freemasonry.

He said that his speech aimed to provoke a debate "which could become the starting point for a movement of reorganization seemingly so sorely needed by our Institution." Then he explained that there were two forms of Masonry:

Ideal Masonry, which exists only in the minds of Masons, encapsulating the highest, most praiseworthy and beautiful aspirations, [and] *real Masonry, which is unfortunately the only kind that truly exists.* [He defined it] *as a society of men admitted through certain ceremonies to take part in periodic meetings, where the most wide-ranging issues are discussed.* [These members] *practice solidarity through benevolent works* [and Masonry] *strives to encourage union between men with a view to peace, concord and universal harmony.*

He then tackled the second theme: Masonic symbolism, which was relevant to the revision of the rituals taking place at the time.

[He defined it as] *a collection of signs, emblems and ceremonies, with a meaning, the knowledge of which is revealed by initiation. Understood in this way, it is the tangible image, the real form of an abstract thought. It represents ideas absolutely in writing, and is even the first method used by men to perpetuate among themselves the truths that they consider useful to pass to their descendants. In this connection, symbolism even offers considerable advantages over ordinary writing, because whilst writing can give rise to dogmatic intolerance, symbolism*

allows independent thought, since it lends itself to free interpretation by the individual. Yet Masonry is universalist and asks only that the novice be free of vulgar prejudices, that he be of good morals, that is of good faith and sincerely devoted to the wellbeing of his fellows. [The essence of the symbol is that it unites man, and that the teaching enclosed within it is not self-evident. It must be sought.] *The majority of Masons have lost the key to the philosophical interpretation of symbols, which for some has become a respectable memory in the form of tradition, and for others a bothersome and obsolete obstacle, at the very best good to captivate the naive intelligence of our fathers, but certainly unworthy of the modern-day emancipated mind.*

This explained his desire to dissociate a political Masonry (which would act on the masses and organize itself accordingly) from a Western initiation based on symbolism (which would educate the elite of humanity). This was a powerful concept, which he returned to constantly, asking the GLDF to train thinkers and the GODF, with its big battalions, to act on a political and social level.

The new official rituals of the French Rite of the GODF, recommended but not obligatory, were known as the "Amiable rituals" and were communicated to the Lodges at the start of 1888. Amiable justified and explained the changes: The physical trials were replaced by a historical and retrospective description. Any mysterious, terrifying or purifying elements were removed. The meaning of the three journeys was rational and progressive. The swords were no longer a symbol of vengeance, but of loyal combat.

Reading the rituals, we can see that the initiation ceremony is much diminished, deprived of any poetry. Among other things, it lacks the four elements, the cadaver, and the bitter cup. It is limited to questions preceding the three journeys, with a choice of possible questions to be asked of the new entrants. Some of these are acceptable, while others are more questionable, such as their opinion on freedom of thought. The three journeys are meant to represent the three ascending stages of life, and the content of the commentaries is basic and essentially moralizing.

An advocate of Masonic education

Wirth, who had become Secretary of the *Amis Triomphants* in January, made a speech on these new rituals on February 7, 1888, entitled *L'initiation adonhiramite et les nouveaux rituels du GODF* ("Adonhiramite initiation and the new rituals of the GODF"). The Lodge Secretary's report makes for interesting reading:[4]

The speaker recognizes the need for a revision of the books of the Symbolic Degrees, but he finds the modifications in the new rituals completely inadequate. He considers them a clumsy half-measure, a hybrid solution, which under the pretext of reconciling all demands, can only lead to generalized discontent. He would have preferred a serious and radical reform, ridding Masonic symbolism of all elements related to Kabbalistic occultism, to leave only the art of building. It would be a work of purification, which could only benefit our Institution, given that this would make it sufficiently clear and intelligible, as well as bringing its practices into line with its own inclinations. Brother Wirth thus urges the Masons to renounce any pretensions they may have to be the successors, today's representatives of the ancient initiates. However, he bases this advice on views which

are not very flattering for the majority of his Brothers. It is not because he finds occult symbolism ridiculous and absurd that he invites Masons to reject it. It is in fact because he thinks the esoteric meaning of this symbolism offers philosophical views so far above the abilities of most Masons that he deigns to judge them unworthy of true initiation, or at least incapable of achieving it. He offers as proof of this the publication of the new rituals, by which the highest dignitaries of the Masonic hierarchy have supposedly proven the utter worthlessness of their initiatory training.

Brother Wirth gives the following motivations for his considerations. He insists that French Masonry needs to renounce the initiation which forces upon it rules it has no concern to follow, and which, ultimately become just a vain pretext for ridiculously gaudy cords and grotesquely pompous titles. He calls for Masons to stick to their sphere and not concern themselves with matters outside their competence. Give back to Caesar what belongs to Caesar, and to the true initiates this occult symbolism that you do not understand and which is far too great for your smallness. Focus on putting into practice the excellent advice given to you by Brother Doumer in his remarkable closing speech from the last Convent. You will observe that it is not a matter of symbolism that you do not know what to do with when it no longer involves the theoretical and practical study of occultism; it is a matter of examining political and social reforms which are suitable to bring into our profane institutions. Your tastes and your aptitudes lead you, my Brothers, toward positive, visible and palpable things. So leave to others the abstract speculations of a transcendent and elusive metaphysics whose rituals contain the mysterious teaching, unbeknownst to you.

---

[4] This account (in French) is published in full in: *1809–2009 Deux siècles d'une loge dans son histoire Athena-Les Amis Triomphants* (GODF Library).

As for the rituals which offend you in their initiatory form, decide to respect them as they were by considering them venerable monuments of philosophical archaeology, or modify them radically, so that they no longer contain anything that is not absolutely logical and in line with your principles. But in the name of good sense, do not accept, disguised as ritual, an imposed and incoherent wild notion which discredits you in the eyes of educated people. Return to your sense of dignity, serious men that you should be, stop devoting yourselves with comical gravity to bizarre procedures which make you ridiculous. With the old rituals, you could hold your heads high in the face of mockery, because you could rightfully consider those who mocked you to be profanes, whose frivolous ignorance could not access the hidden meaning of your mysteries. But today, with your new rituals, you can only hang your head, lamenting the forever lost word, as your third Degree teaches you.

The Worshipful Master Vidau could only voice "strong reservations" about such proposals. Wirth answered that in Masonic matters, he seemed to speak for an opportunism which he would certainly deny in political matters. In fact, he was highly anticlerical, and in 1891 he founded a league to suppress the budget of cults. A battery of thanks was given in his honor, after the Worshipful Master unwisely decided to call upon other Lodges to continue the discussion.

The second debate took place on March 6, in the presence of two Councilors of the Order, and above all Esprit-Eugène Hubert,[5] the director of the *Chaîne d'Union*. Then the review gave an account of the meeting at the *Amis Triomphants* Lodge on April 3, 1888, on the same theme: *Adonhiramite initiation and the new rituals of the GODF*. Wirth defended the beauty and knowledge of old Masonry, while asserting that he regarded it as "a web of reveries and pipedreams." Brother Armand Lévy, 33rd degree, dignitary of the SCDF, of the *Mont Sinaï* Lodge, a man of outstanding character who was close to Prince Napoleon and behind the sending of a workers' delegation to the Universal Exhibition of London, supported him, but asserted that Masonry was founded by Moses (perhaps because of the ten commandments).

Conversely, A.S. Morin, a man of letters and a publicist, Municipal Councilor of Paris and former Worshipful Master of *La Clémente Amitié*, saw the ritual as nothing more than a means of self-protection under the despotic regimes, but which had lost its purpose. The comments of the last speaker, Doctor Gonnard, 33rd degree, member of the *Philanthropes Réunis* Lodge (SCDF), and future Lieutenant Grand Commander, are interesting for anyone seeking to understand the point of view of a dignitary of the Scottish Rite. He thought that nobody took the symbols seriously any more, but that they should be maintained as a means of protection and a diplomatic language within universal Masonry, and because without them, Masonry would disappear. In other words, it was necessary to uphold these customs in order for the SCDF to preserve its international relations with the other European Supreme Councils. During one of the sessions, Amiable, present at the Orient, was invited by the Worshipful Master to speak about the rituals (of which

---

[5] Esprit-Eugène Hubert, born in 1819, former prefecture councilor and publicist, Head of the Secretariat of the Grand Orient. He was relieved of his duties by Prince Murat in 1853 for disciplinary and unofficially political reasons. He was director of the Masonic review *La Chaîne d'Union* in 1869, a deist and a republican, and highly attached to the reference to the GAOTU.

he had written the greater part). He declined, because, he said, he had not attended Wirth's conference.

It seems that there was another reason for Wirth, to whom Vidau had offered such a fine opportunity, choosing to depart. He demanded that those aspiring to the Degrees of Fellow and Master present a work on their Masonic knowledge, whereas Vidau, for fear of hostile reactions, wanted this work (which had not yet entered Masonic customs) to be optional. However, Wirth did not show too much hostility to his old Lodge. According to his famous joke, he left it to triumph without him, because in 1894, he returned to propose the organization of a Masonic celebration paying homage to the defeated men of Thermidor (Wirth showed particular interest in the life of clubs under the Revolution), and, at the GLSE, he was one of the three guarantors of friendship with the GODF. He attended the opening of the first GODF Museum, and after consulting Stanislas de Guaita, enjoyed commenting on the meanings of the four major symbolic paintings in *La Revue Maçonnique*. In the first issue of *Le Symbolisme*, in 1912, he recognized the precursory merit of Antoine Blatin, former Grand Commander of the GCDR who had resisted the "devastating current which seemed to want to destroy everything of the old Masonic traditions" with "unshakable tenacity" after the 1883 Convent.[6]

Wirth at the *Grande Loge Symbolique Écossaise*

Marius Lepage tells us that Wirth joined the *Philanthropes Réunis* (SCDF), certainly upon invitation from Doctor Gonnard, but that it did not suit him. By chance, leaving the Lodge, he met Ferdinand Baudel, a former Communard, deported to Nouméa in New Caledonia, liberated in 1879, and (it seems) initiated in 1882 to the *Travail et Vrais Amis Fidèles* (*TVAF*) Lodge, n°5, a Lodge of the GLSE. The two of them debated about Masonry, its rites and its symbolism, and found they had common ground.[7]

This dissident Obedience, uniting around 25 Lodges and founded in 1880, was the result of a schism provoked by the refusal of the reforms asked of the SCDF, at the time led by Adolphe Crémieux, for reasons of international recognition. The new Obedience was very liberal, and practiced the Scottish Rite without imposing the GAOTU. It did not include any High Degrees. This did not bother Oswald Wirth, who considered that coming from the building trades and based on constructivism, Masonry could stop at the Degree of Master. He was admitted to the 4th and 14th Degrees of the Ancient and Accepted Scottish Rite, upon invitation from Charles Limousin, but without any motivation, and was pushed by his friend Albert Lantoine to the 33rd Degree, without really applying himself.

---

[6] In 1910, in *La Lumière maçonnique*, he congratulated himself on the promotion of his successor Gaston Bouley, who had reached the High Degrees of the SCDF, and must have been disappointed to learn that unlike Blatin, he had opposed the invocation of the GAOTU in the new ritual of the Rectified Scottish Rite.
[7] In the eulogy that he wrote for the 25th anniversary of his initiation, Wirth tells us that Baudel was a classmate of Gambetta at the Collège de Cahors, that during the Commune, he was almost shot by the Versaillais then by the Communards, who mistook him for a priest in disguise. He was arrested by the Versaillais after fighting on a barricade near the Porte de Romainville.

This new Obedience was led by high class politicians such as Charles Floquet, Henri Brisson and Gustave Mesureur. It was at the forefront of the combat against Boulangism, and its ranks included atheist Masons and other spiritualists, as well as a few staunch supporters of mixed Lodges. It had a *Bulletin* which Wirth used to voice his views. In 1891, to widen its influence, this *Bulletin* became *Le Bulletin maçonnique, organe de la Franc-Maçonnerie universelle* ("The Masonic Bulletin, Organ of Universal Freemasonry") then in 1895, *La Revue maçonnique, organe de la Franc-maçonnerie française et étrangère* ("The Masonic Review, Organ of French and Foreign Freemasonry"). From the first issue, it announced the publications of the *Société magnétique de France* (French Magnetic Society), gave accounts of feminist congresses, and allowed a controversy to develop between one of its editors, Paul Schäfer, and the magician Papus (who was not yet a Mason), on the subject of symbolism and ritual. In 1892, elected to the Executive Committee of the GLSE, Wirth was president of the *Commission des règlements généraux et particuliers* (Commission of general and specific regulations), took part in the committee on rituals, and like Baudel who was elected later, could have more influence over its orientations. Sometimes he was unsuccessful, for example in 1894, when he proposed the formation of a Council of Masters, to be the philosophical Council of the Rite. All the same, his views could certainly be more easily understood and taken into account in a small liberal structure than in a large monolithic Obedience like the GODF.

In November 1888, he was still at the *Amis Triomphants* when, invited by Baudel,

he spoke at *TVAF* on "ancient initiations and the origins of Freemasonry." During the same meeting, the Worshipful Master Achille Cesbron, a painter who helped to decorate the Hôtel de Ville in Paris, spoke about the future democratic constitution. That month, the Lodge initiated Gaston da Costa (1850–1909), another former Communard, who had been sentenced to death, pardoned, then deported to New Caledonia, and had become a Boulangist socialist. In 1889, he published a new method for teaching French grammar. The sculptor Gabriel Chalon, a third former Communard and Lieutenant in the National Guard, who had similarly been deported, was also initiated into *TVAF* and became a fervent supporter of Wirth.

We know some of the agendas of this Lodge, which it sometimes sent to the *Bulletin hebdomadaire des Loges de la Région parisienne* ("Weekly Bulletin of Lodges of the Parisian Region"). This allows us to follow some of its activities from 1889 to 1896, when it joined the new Grande Loge de France. *TVAF*, which had (and would only ever have) around 20 to 30 members, sometimes struggled to bring together seven Masters, and although it was influenced by Wirth, he was far from being its "guru" as Jean Baylot thought.[8]

On December 25, 1888, Baudel spoke on "The origin and the goals of Freemasonry." This gave rise to a debate between Wirth and a certain Muret, concerning the Masonic Degrees. A battery of joy was given in honor of Henri-Blaise Chassaing (1855–1908), his former delegate Worshipful Master at the GLSE, and of Alfred Martineau (1859–1945). Both were elected to the Chamber of Deputies in October 1880, one being a radical, and the other a Boulangist socialist. In 1893, Martineau, a

---

[8] Jean Baylot's study, *Oswald Wirth 1860–1943 rénovateur et mainteneur de la Véritable Franc-Maçonnerie*, (Paris: Dervy-Livres, 1975), 239 p., is the most complete biography of Wirth to date.

graduate of the École des Chartes, entered the Higher Council of the Colonies, and it was possibly on his recommendation that in 1897, Wirth obtained his job as a librarian at the Ministry of Colonies.

In January 1889, the Lodge voted for initiations to follow the ancient rituals, but without specifying which, and profanes were subject to symbolic tests, explained and commented upon by Oswald Wirth. However, Wirth did not request membership until February 12, 1889, and received it on March 26. In June 1889, Da Costa's speech for his salary increase to the Degree of Fellow was on the subject: "Dictatorship. Can it be legitimate?" This was connected to his Blanquist past. In October, with Chassaing, Rey and Da Costa, Wirth registered to participate in a debate on the organization of universal suffrage.

TVAF held bimonthly meetings or committees, for Masonic training or internal affairs. It was unusual in that it regularly held open meetings. Given the extreme smallness of the headquarters on Rue Payenne, where the positivist church had recently still presided, these had to be limited to a few dozen profane guests. Thus, on March 8, 1890, Oswald Wirth explained the interest of these open meetings from a propaganda point of view, Brother Bertrand spoke on Masonic socialism, and Chassaing on the order of lawyers. Then Wirth spoke on Freemasonry and fraternity among peoples. The two other subjects concerned mass education and the current situation. In June, attendees heard three speakers:

Brother Bertrand on socialism and Masonry, Da Costa on the odyssey of a convicted criminal, and Armand Lévy on the burning of Joan of Arc. It was then decided that two out of three subjects should be Masonic, and the third should target profanes.

In 1891, Wirth spoke on therapeutic magnetism, Baudel spoke on the origins of Masonry, and Talon addressed the issue of one-off and progressive tax. In 1893, attendees witnessed a hypnotism session, Laurent Tailhade[9] spoke on occultism in contemporary literature, and a poem (by Wirth?) on the Great Work was recited. In 1894, Laurent Tailhade spoke on pity in contemporary drama, the future patriarch of the Gnostic Church, Fabre des Essarts,[10] talked about children's rights, and there was a discussion on mysticism between Wirth and Ledrain, a teacher at the École du Louvre. However, each contributor had just 20 minutes, separated by artistic intervals with students from the Conservatoire, so none of these themes could have been developed in depth.

At the final open meeting of 1895, Ledrain spoke on the Gospels, Charles Limousin,[11] who had become a close friend of Wirth, spoke on Freemasonry, and Eugène Fournière, a socialist intellectual close to Benoît Malon, discussed its social role. In 1900, Charles Limousin addressed the subject of "the religion of Freemasonry" and Oswald Wirth tackled that of "Islam and the religious brotherhoods." These conferences continued at the GLDF during the First World War.

---

[9] Laurent Tailhade (1854–1919), poet, friend of Verlaine, and anarchist pamphleteer.

[10] Léonce Fabre des Essarts (1848–1917), publicist and poet, and Fourierist. He was one of the first Gnostic bishops consecrated by Jules Doinel. He consecrated René Guénon and Jean Bricaud as Patriarchs. In 1893, he was a member of the *La Rose du Parfait Silence* Lodge (GODF).

[11] Charles Limousin (1840–1909), Fourierist, Parisian leader of the First International, and conciliator under the Commune. A publicist, he led the fight in favor of cooperative and mutualist movements under the Second Empire and the Third Republic. He was initiated in 1869 by Scottish Lodge 133 (*La Justice*) after two failures in other Lodges. He did not follow the dissidence of the GLSE and reached the 33rd Degree in the SCDF.

In 1890, Achille Cesbron was maintained as Worshipful Master of *TVAF*. Baudel was elected First Surveillant, and Wirth, Second Surveillant. This gave him the responsibility of training the Apprentices. Pasquier, General Secretary of the French Federation of Free Thinking was Orator, and the deputy Martineau was Secretary. Although the Lodge had left-wing leanings, both currents (spiritualist with Baudel and Wirth, and atheist with Pasquier and Martineau) were represented there. The works were sometimes Masonic, and sometimes social or societal. Wirth and Baudel specialized in initiatory subjects. One gave a speech on Masonic symbolism and science, and the other dealt with the theme, "What is an Initiate?"

In 1891, Pasquier was elected Worshipful Master, replacing Cesbron. Baudel and Wirth kept their positions as Surveillants and Da Costa became Orator. Among the speeches that captured attention were those of Fabre des Essarts, on "the revolutionary mind in the Church" and of Wirth on "magic and magnetism." In 1892, Cesbron took the First Gavel, while Wirth and Baudel exchanged their Surveillant's boards. The Lodge dealt with the subjects of the Austro-German influence in the Balkans and clericalism. Da Costa took an interest in women in the civil service, particularly female teachers; in December, *TVAF* addressed the question: should Masons who voted for the budget of cults be condemned? But it was Vidau, former Worshipful Master of the Amis Triomphants who led the fight. Wirth asked the question again at the GLSE meeting: should they be condemned for "betrayal of their legislative mandate." The matters meant to have been treated during the year by the Lodge included the social role of Masonry, Masonry and the Society of Jesus, cremation, and the scientific situation of magnetic forces.

Wirth became a Worshipful Master in 1893. He asked *TVAF* to participate in the subscription for his friend Abbot Roca, a dissident preacher, esotericist and social Christian, "persecuted by the Church because of his liberal publications," but the Abbot died that year. The themes debated included the Masonic Kabbalah (by Charles Limousin), religious evolution in various human races, and the role of Freemasonry in the face of clerical threats. The aim was to study the organization of democracy, political clubs, their action on universal suffrage and the control they could exert over national representation. Wirth gave the Light to the future "traitor" Jean-Baptiste Bidegain, who was a sales representative at the time.

In 1894, the Lodge was under the gavel of Baudel. In May, a certain Lévy presented the works of the ex-Abbot Constant, former Mason and author of magic rituals. Bidegain presented his initiatory impressions, then asked: Should Freemasonry fight religious sentiment? He claimed to be a materialist, but said that "sentiment is like the synthesis of what is noblest and highest within us." He then spoke on the subject: What is Freemasonry?

In 1895, still Worshipful Master, Baudel was lyrical in his words:

It is in the bosom of our Lodge that, for six years, the ideas preparing to conquer all Freemasonry, and subsequently through it, the whole world, have been maturing. The extinguished flame of the philosophical traditions of our Order has been reignited in our midst. It is given to us to find the lost word...

In January, the Lodge debated philosophical conceptions to replace clerical dogmatism. It discussed the soul and the next life, as well as atheism and the anarchist movement.

Wirth and Baudel began to gain a reputation outside of their Lodge. Thus, on April 3, 1890, Wirth spoke at *La Ligne Droite* (SCDF) on "Freemasonry made intelligible to its members." In 1891, at the *Amis de la Patrie* (GODF) he spoke on symbolism as a means of victorious combat against obscurantism and superstition. He also spoke on symbolism to *L'Esprit moderne* (GODF) and to the Rite of Misraim. He spoke at the *Le Buisson ardent et les Pyramides* Lodge, on the meaning of the expression ALGDGADLU ("In the Name of the Great Architect of the Universe") and the reasons for its continued use, and to the *Arc-en-ciel* and to Misraïm, on alchemy and on Freemasonry.

However, the message was primarily transmitted through the Obedience's review. In July 1889, in this publication, Wirth gave an account of the international Masonic Congress, which took place on Rue Cadet on the centenary of the Revolution, and where he had the opportunity to give a very brief speech. In his report, where he praises Amiable's contribution, he calls for union, and again attributes the rupture of the GODF with the Anglo-Saxon Obediences not to the abolition of a dogmatic affirmation (God and the immortality of the soul), but to the disappearance of the formula ALGDGADLU: "In the Name of the Great Architect of the Universe." The November and December 1889 issues of the GLSE's *Bulletin Maçonnique* featured the text of a Lodge conference on the theme of "Freemasonry and politics." The January 1891 bulletin asked "Is Freemasonry of religion?" The March and April issues 1892 addressed "Masonic science." The February 1893 bulletin examined "The truth about the Rose-Croix" and symbolism.

In these fundamental articles, Wirth returns to several essential ideas, but formulates them skillfully and differently.

He writes:

> *Until now, Masons have only demolished. They have furiously attacked the unstable edifice of a discredited cult. The aim is no longer to scatter or pulverize its materials. Instead, we must learn to use them, to integrate them into the facade of the magnificent Sanctuary that Masons must build to the truth as it is revealed alive to human reason…* [He adds that] *we are not living in an anti-religious era, but only one that criticizes the symbolic forms that disguise its sublime character.* [He wants this new sanctuary to replace] *cunning, shameful and perverse clericalism which wants to dominate the world by keeping the people in systematic ignorance…* [He defines Masonry as] *the ultimate religion, that is, the indestructible connection that unites all individuals and all peoples under the aegis of the sacred laws of justice and solidarity, so well represented by the emancipating trilogy: Liberty, Equality, Fraternity […]. This single universal religion that all people await as the promised Messiah, in the form of multiple allegories.*

In *La Franc-Maçonnerie est-elle une religion?* ("Is Freemasonry a religion?"), he adds that it is the absolute opposite, because it aspires to free minds without suppressing consciousness, and without the tyranny of a dogma. With its tolerance, practical cult of solidarity, fervent love for humanity and glorification of work (but not as "the punishment for an imaginary fault of our first forebears"), it is the "true religion." This hope of creating a new religion on Masonic foundations was not new, but it came up against two obstacles: the variety of philosophical and spiritual choices among Masons, and the very character of the Institution, which was closed to profanes.

In *La Science maçonnique*, the Royal Art is defined as the art of universal construction, and the GAOTU as "the principle of unity of the great everything, a coordinating impulse of general harmony." We can also observe a few elegant phrases on initiation, "which imposes nothing but seeks to guide" and an explanation which is repeated in his works on initiation and the symbols. He wants to make Masonry "the unviolated asylum of wisdom," united by "mutual tolerance" and "a shared sentiment of fraternity" (on this, he cites the words of Abbot Rocca). It must therefore remove questions of "narrow politics" from its works. He calls again for a split of Masonic forces "between the brain, for discernment and thought" and the hand for action. In 1893, he expressed concern that Masons might abandon the domain of pure speculation to theologians, because "clericalism is working" to "renew its antiquated dogmatism and will soon present it in a form so transfigured that many will be fooled."

The Masonic Group for Initiatory Studies, Ritual and the *Book of the Apprentice*

During the year 1889, *TVAF* (mostly Wirth and Baudel) founded a Masonic Group for Initiatory Studies with the Worshipful Master Cesbron as president. The secretary was a certain Ogi (possibly a pseudonym), member of the hermetic Rose-Croix society. He was an unknown Superior of the Martinist Initiation, and therefore close to Papus, but his name does not reappear after this. The group wanted to write a work entitled: *La Franc-Maçonnerie rendue intelligible aux Francs-Maçons* ("Freemasonry made intelligible to Freemasons") and published a 76-page booklet, written and illustrated by Wirth. The work was completed in 1892, and with Wirth present, the trials of a project for an "interpretive ritual for the Degree of Apprentice" were submitted to the GLSE at the session of November 28, 1892, with a request that it be examined and submitted to the Obedience's Lodges for study. The GLSE agreed for the ritual to be examined, but refused to impose it. They said that the GLSE's executive committee would ensure it was transmitted to French Obediences, and that the Lodge was free to send it to other foreign Obediences. In June 1893, three copies of the rituals were sent to the Lodges of the GLSE, under the aegis of the Masonic Group for Initiatory Studies.

This ritual was trialed at *Travail et Vrais Amis Fidèles*, and in 1892, it was used for an initiation ceremony at *Union et Bienfaisance* (SCDF). In 1891, in the *Bulletin maçonnique*, the Lodge announced that four "passionate and highly educated" apprentices had been promoted to the Degree of Fellow, after being questioned about their Masonic knowledge, and that after the ceremony, "they received the instruction of the Degree, in line with the ancient ritual of the GODF" (the *Régulateur* of 1801?). The symbols were then explained to them, giving rise to the developments on the flaming star, and subsequently on gnosis, the theories of the Rose-Croix and the esotericism of religions in general.

The foreword to the new ritual outlines the admissibility conditions: in the Chamber of Reflection, the profane is asked about his duties to men, to himself, and to his fellows (not to God or his country), and the testament he must write is a moral one. The opening of the works of the Lodge is very simple and does not mention the GAOTU. The applicant is interrogated, with a focus on Masonry or on the uncomfortable situation in which it finds itself, then he receives several explanations, before undergoing the traditional tests. Every journey represents situations: the first is "the darkness of the North," followed by purification by water and more questions, the second is the learning of the knowledge, followed by the flames, and the third makes him an initiate after the test of the bitter cup. The formula of reception is "In the Name of Universal Freemasonry." The closing of the works is succinct. A high-quality ritual, worthy of the Institution and without embellishment.

The Masonic Group for Initiatory Studies announced the publications of the *Livre de l'apprenti* ("Book of the Apprentice"), a manual for new initiates, of *Alchimie et la Franc-Maçonnerie* ("Alchemy and Freemasonry") (with studies on the origins of Masonry and on symbolism to represent the principles of a rational philosophy) and *L'Église et la Franc-Maçonnerie, une lettre adressée au pape par un initié* ("The Church and Freemasonry, a Letter from an Initiate to the Pope"). Work on the interpretive ritual for the Degree of Fellow and the *Book of the Fellow* was underway.

The reception of the ritual was "rather discouraging," whereas the *Book of the Apprentice*, published in 1894, immediately had a degree of success. It begins with a "philosophical glance at the general history of Freemasonry" (which could luckily be corrected by further research), followed by an overview of the Masonic situation in France and abroad, and developments on initiation. The cover page indicates that in the book, "the initiatory rites are interpreted philosophically for the first time." There is a chapter devoted to "the philosophical conceptions connected with the ritualism of the Degree of Apprentice," with a bold comment: "it compares old ideas to modern discoveries, which confirm them in the most unexpected fashion." This is followed by sections on the duties of the Apprentice and an interpretive catechism of this Degree.

Masonry is cautiously defined as "a universal alliance of enlightened men, united to work together towards the intellectual and moral perfection of humanity." The work ends with some "first elements of an

initiatory philosophy," with a description of the Temple and an explanation of the various symbols. The conclusion of the publicity booklet sent to the Lodges is filled with self-satisfaction for having helped to "greatly elevate the intellectual level of our Order." It claims that this book "allows the Lodges to be relieved of their responsibility to educate their members" and to "truly enlighten new initiates." This slightly modified manual of the Apprentice, which today might seem very dated in form and content, was recently revisited by Irène Mainguy. It has been a reference text and a recommended work for many new Masons in all Obediences, even up to today. *TVAF* would publish the *Book of the Fellow* in 1912 and the *Book of the Master* in 1922.

The Initiation of Women

In June 1890, three years before the creation of the *Droit Humain* Lodge, the Lodge held a contradictory debate on the admission of women. After the creation of this first mixed Lodge, Wirth, elected to the bodies of the GLSE, asked on February 12, 1894 for his Lodge to be authorized to receive *Droit Humain* members (implying both male and female), with the following expectations:

Considering that Freemasonry has a duty to prevent women being influenced by obscurantism, and that the best way of doing this is to make the Masonic light shine in their eyes.

Considering, moreover, its recent creation in Paris, allowing the initiation of women, the TVAF Lodge asks the GLSE for its authorization to admit members of the mixed Droit Humain Lodge to its works.

The TVAF Lodge thus proposes to conduct an experiment which might enlighten

Freemasonry, and subsequently give it a fully informed appreciation of the advantages and disadvantages of the definitive admission of women into Freemasonry.

Predictably, this request was refused, because the GLSE feared isolation, and the debate on mixed Lodges returned at *TVAF* in 1894 with the questions: "Can Masonry disregard female intellectuality? Should women be initiated? What initiation is suitable?" Should we see this last question as favoring Lodges of Adoption, a way of countering the campaign to allow women within the GLDF? In February 1899, asked about the *Droit Humain* Lodge, he answered that as far as he knew its works were initiatory, which was sufficient. In a letter to André Lebey, on April 30, 1923, he refused to consider "the weaknesses of women, which we can assume to be known," took an initiatory standpoint and asked: "In her own intelligence, will she find enough conspiratorial spirit to join an association which pursues a very long-term program of human regeneration?"[12]

The Amiable Affair

After studying the rituals and the *Book of the Apprentice*, Louis Amiable, Grand Orator of the GCDR, concluded that Wirth's goal was to "bring Masonry back to religiosity, to give it an almost confessional nature, while waiting for the movement in this direction to be specified in the written work announced to be in preparation: *L'Église et la Franc-Maçonnerie, étude impartiale dédié au pape par un initié* ("The Church and Freemasonry: an impartial study dedicated to the Pope by an initiate"). At the same time, the author worked to make this Institution ridiculous

by assimilating it with the old alchemy… Wirth, he wrote, can now address the Pope with confidence. He will be well-received, as were Léo Taxil and Rosen, and as Jules Doinel will be. This was the understandable reaction of a rationalist who feared that Wirth's writings might strengthen a Masonic form of obscurantism. Also understandable was Wirth's anger, when he had other things to worry about. He was the victim of a Kabbalah in the occultist circles, and was suffering with an illness of the spinal cord.

The error of judgment is obvious. Like the Masons of his generation, Wirth was anticlerical and simply said that there was no incompatibility between religious belief and Masonic membership. This is far removed from the letter to the Supreme Pontificate!

Wirth was a Mason through and through, whereas Rosen was a conman, Taxil was a vile joker, perhaps unaware of the consequences that would later come of his pranks, and Jules Doinel, former GODF Councilor of the Order and founder of the Gnostic Church, had serious psychological problems. The report had been sent confidentially to the presidents of the Lodges, to warn them, and the Lodge made a complaint against Amiable, but he died in 1897. To leave it there, let us simply say that Amiable perhaps even did Wirth a favor, by making his work known.

Insights on Wirth and *Travail et Vrais Amis Fidèles* within the GLDF (1896–1914)

It is important to remember that the Supreme Council, under pressure from Lodges in the north of France, gave autonomy to its symbolic Lodges through a decree of November 7, 1894. This allowed a French Grand Lodge, the *Grande Loge de*

---

[12] "Il y dix ans, le Symbolisme," *Chroniques d'Histoire Maçonnique* 55: 109.

France, to be born. Then, in a second stage, it renounced the right to deliver patents to the newly formed Lodges. These concessions and the resolution of financial issues allowed the majority of GLSE Lodges to enter the new Obedience. In an initial version, this Obedience defined Masonry as "a universal alliance based on solidarity, to promote the success of all emancipatory evolutions."

TVAF voted for the principle of adhesion to the GLDF on December 11, 1894 and this took effect in 1896. Concerning the question of the GAOTU, the Supreme Council decided to make this invocation optional, and therefore not part of the rituals. It was to be maintained in patents delivered by the Supreme Council and in overseas Lodges. The Grand Commander Raymond defined it as "the universal synthesis." The debate resumed in 1903 within the GLDF. Baudel defended it in a meeting of the Grand Lodge as a "manifestation of our tolerance towards all beliefs, rising against the absolutism of dogmas." In conclusion, it was decided that the formula would feature in the rituals of the Symbolic Lodges, but would not be imposed.

This decision did not disturb the life of *TVAF*, now n°137. In 1896, it studied the brochure of the Grand Master of the Swiss Grand Lodge Alpina on "propaganda for peace," and received Papus as Sovereign Commander of the Martinist Order. He spoke on Martinism and its connections with Masonry.

In 1897, with Baudel holding the gavel, the Lodge affiliated former Blanquist Communard Alphonse Humbert, who had been deported to New Caledonia and become a radical socialist deputy. It tackled the subjects of the powerlessness of evolutionary theories, the imposition of hands, and philosopher's medicine, but also the exclusion of Masonry from clerically inclined parliaments, and the sending of a delegation to the Freethinking Congress. Moreover, a contradictory debate was opened on the question of anti-Semitism, which had become a subject of discussion as the Dreyfuss affair began to increase public awareness. Later, any anti-Semitic statement made in the Lodge would be subject to indictment.

A remarkable study by Paul Lanchais[13] tells us that on July 13, 1897 the debate on the social question brought Baudel (who wanted to limit the action of the Lodge to the education of its members) and Brother Guerrier (who thought that Masonry should concern itself with the well-being of humanity and the liberation of the citizen) into opposition. Were these signs of a future conflict on orientation? Pasquier was elected Worshipful Master then fell ill, so was replaced in June 1898 by Wirth, who was re-elected in November. Eight Brothers, including Pasquier, resigned. This made it easier for Wirth to impose his line. In December, he invited his Lodge to follow the rights to the letter, but while seeking to understand their meaning. In 1900, the Lodge debated the reform of Scottish ritualism.

In a report addressed to the GLDF in December 1901, according to the Secretary, the Lodge considered that:

Freemasonry should step back from profane occupations, concerning itself only with the superior interests of humanity. It must rise above political questions, and not forget that it is not just French, but universal. It is for these reasons that the works of Lodges must be primarily philosophical.

The program of works for our Lodge is taken from the symbolism of our Institution in the form of the questions: "Where do we

---

[13] Paul Lanchais, *Cahiers de la Loge Silence* (1975, available at the GLDF library).

come from, where are we going, who are we?" *We have undertaken to study these questions, which are of vital importance to resolve the great problem of a universal religion and morality based entirely on feeling and reason.*

These studies are relevant, because we are undergoing a period of religious and moral renovation. The old religions are exhausted, intelligence guided by science is moving towards another religion, another morality, better adapted to our needs. It is this religion, this morality that we Masons have a duty to research and establish. We must make every effort to resolve the problem and find a satisfactory solution. We believe that this is the goal that Freemasonry must achieve, as an institution of philosophy and a mutual school of instruction and improvement...

The Lodge held a solemn session and committee meeting for initiatory training, open to visiting Brothers. It had 23 active members. Attendance was sometimes poor, and the opening of the works was problematic. The Secretary outlined the series of subjects tackled in 1901:

The spirit of philosophical research and dogmatism, spiritualism and materialism, the origins of the alphabet, psychic phenomena and their interpretation, the participation of women in the work of Freemasonry, Lodges of Adoption, the Pax League, the concentration camps in the Transvaal, symbolism and Masonic insignia, symbolism and the influence of environments, religions opposed to Freemasonry, where do we come from?

In 1901, Wirth was admitted to the Federal Council of the GLDF via an election, and was responsible for the Obedience's library. He was in charge of "drafting the works" of the Council in 1903,

but intervened very little. When he did, it was to advocate a return to the old ritual of the SCDF for the Degree of Fellow. He remained silent during the debate on the question of the GAOTU.

In 1903, the *TVAF* Worshipful Master was the painter Henri Bonis. He was then replaced by Baudel. Then Wirth alternated the holding of the First Gavel with other Brothers. In 1904, the Lodge examined the esotericism of the Degree of Rose-Croix, and Martineau spoke on indigenous colonization in Comoros. A mourning battery was given in memory of Louise Michel. In 1906, Da Costa was looking for a philosophical orientation for Freemasonry. In 1908, Wirth spoke on symbolism among the first Knights and Pierre Piobb discussed initiatory geometry.

As deputy at the GLDF Convent in 1906, Wirth began refusing to vote for any political vow. He therefore abstained from that following the legislative elections in 1906, by which the GLDF paid homage to the minister Combes and "invited the current government to take inspiration from this glorious example in the rigorous application of the law of separation, and above all in the implementation of the economic and social reforms that it has promised to democracy and the working class." Only three Lodges supported his point of view and consequently abstained from voting in favor of the Duma, following the 1905 Russian Revolution.

In 1902, with the appearance of *L'Acacia*, a review edited by Charles Limousin, Wirth found an opportunity to extend his audience. The two men conducted a debate on the GAOTU and Wirth reassured his friend that: "there can be no doubt in my mind: just because a Mason will not believe in God, this does not make him a profane in an apron." Aside from these traditional themes on symbolism, the mysteries, alchemy or hermeticism, he took an interest in foreign Masonries, which also needed to be "regenerated." He gave his point of view on North American and German Masons, was critical regarding over-politicized French Masonry, but also about Anglo-Saxon masonry, which clung to "pompous ceremony," that the Brothers "practice with the regularity of robots, without worrying their heads about the possible esoteric significance of the rites they conduct as meticulous observers of an unheeded text." He preferred German Masonry, which he saw as a role model, because it was careful not to frighten religious minds, supporting them in their faith, "which they refine in light of a very broad humanitarian philosophy." He concluded that "whatever one says, man will remain a religious animal."

In 1905, in an article entitled "The new Polyeucte", he wrote (for the last time?) on a political theme, supporting the anti-militarist action of anarchist teacher, Gustave Hervé,[14] who he considered "honest and sincere," while reproaching him for wanting war between the social classes. His most significant article, published in 1904, was entitled "L'Initiation maçonnique et le Grand Architecte de l'Univers" ("Masonic Initiation and the Great Architect of the Universe"). In it, he attempts to define his understanding of initiation. He writes that it aims to train thinkers and requires people to go deeper, beyond the surface. It is based on reason (Sun J) combined with imagination (Moon B), on the male activity of the mind united with the female receptiveness of intelligence. "It will never be revealed to a reasoner who is not also a seer." Masonic symbolism is portrayed as a harmonic whole encapsulating everything: Mason, Masonry, Architecture, Architect... Masonic initiation proposes, if not to give us a theoretical acquaintance with the Great

Architect... at least to give us the concrete ability to carry out his intentions. In the November 1909 issue of the same review, he defines it as "general intelligence which lies in specific intelligences." The difficulty of defining a symbol!

He later wrote in the monthly *Lumière Maçonnique* which came out in 1910, and which he temporarily managed. Then, in 1912, he founded the review *Le Symbolisme*. The following year, he would be forced to ask for a subsidy from the Federal Council, because this austere review had a deficit of 800 francs. In 1911, his Lodge asked for Masonry to abstain from any profane manifestation, and in 1913, it protested against the custom of smoking in temples. The deputy chosen by *TVAF* in 1912 (there were just 11 voters), Brother Platel, who was elected to the Federal Council of the GLDF, was a syndicalist teacher and an ardent socialist. He helped to persuade the GLDF to adopt socialist and very left-wing political positions. After his death on the front in 1916, Wirth, who had met him at GLDF meetings and at the Federal Council, sent a very moving letter to his widow, evoking the death of his own brother, who died in the line of duty in 1914.

---

[14] At the time, Gustave Hervé, a history teacher, chief editor of *La Guerre Sociale*, was a member of the mixed Lodge *L'Idéal Social*, under the maintained GLSE.

Jinarajadasa (1875-1953): A Bridge Between East and West

Jean Iozia

Jinarajadasa was born on December 16, 1875 in Ceylon (now Sri Lanka), to Sinhalese parents in a village near *Panadura* on the east coast. The island of Ceylon has always been a crossroads where east and west meet, undoubtedly because of its strategic position in the Indian ocean.

Charles Webster Leadbeater (1847–1934), joined the Theosophical Society in 1883. He moved to Colombo in Ceylan in June 1886. Here, he was head of one of the schools created by the theosophists for Sinhalese Buddhist children. It was in this school that Jinarajadasa met Leadbeater for the first time in 1887.

In 1888, Leadbeater offered the young Jinarajadasa the chance of a good education in England. This was the start of a new life for Jinarajadasa. He would discover a new civilization and a different culture. He was thirteen years old. From this moment, Jinarajadasa's life became intertwined with the history of the Theosophical Society.

Jinarajadasa entered St John College's at Cambridge University in 1896. Four years later, he obtained his degree in Sanskrit and philology.[1] He was a talented sportsman, and joined the *Lady Margaret Boat Club*. This was a key moment in his university life. He steered the boat for his college the year it won a quadruple victory.[2]

At the start of 1902, he went to study in Milan for two years at the Academy of Literature and Science, a branch of the famous University of Pavia. He already spoke French, which he had studied, as well as other Latin languages including Spanish and Portuguese.

In January 1912 Annie Besant left for Europe with the young Krishnamurti. She wanted to give this child a good education. Jinarajadasa would be his tutor. He is described as a man of knowledge and culture, quiet and studious, with a soft voice and good manners, despite the great suffering caused by his health problems.[3]

Indian Politics

Annie Besant, President of the Theosophical Society, popularized the *Home Rule League* in India and was very active in Indian politics. However, the English authorities began to see her political activities as dangerous. On June 7, 1917, Annie Besant, B.P. Wadia and George Arundale were placed under house arrest. Jinarajadasa took over as president of the Executive Committee of the Society during their house arrest in Ootacamund.

Nevertheless, in 1917, Annie Besant became president of the *Indian Congress*. In 1933, Jinarajadasa wrote a short work, in which he recalls that he was always closely associated with Annie Besant's political activities aiming to obtain dominion status for India. In it, he describes the main initiatives of this campaign up to 1925, when the *Commonwealth of India Bill* was presented to the Communities.[4]

---

[1] Gregory Tillett, *The Elder Brother, A Biography of Charles Webster Leadbeater* (London: Rouledge & Kegan Paul, 1982), 91.

[2] Rowing, University Boat Race, *Times*, March 1, 1897.

[3] Emily Lutyens, *Candles in The Sun* (London: Rupert Hart-Davis, 1957), 38–39.

[4] Curuppumullage Jinarajadasa, *The Conventions of the Indian Constitution* (Adyar: Theosophical Publishing House, 1933).

doi: 10.18278/rscs.4.1.5

His wife, Dorothy Graham-Jinarajadasa, would help to create women's groups across the whole Indian subcontinent. On May 8, 1917 in Adyar, she launched the *Women's Indian Association.* This movement was one of the first women's movements in India. In 1921, women were granted the right to vote in three Indian states: Madras, Cochin and Travancore. In Cochin and Travancore, they were also eligible for the Legislative Councils.

In 1923, the *Home Rule for India British Auxiliary* changed its name to *The Commonwealth of India League.* The name change motion was suggested by Jinarajadasa. The *Commonwealth of India Bill* was drafted and accepted in 1925. During his trips around Europe,[5] Jinarajadasa continued defending the project for *Home Rule* in India, and called for demonstrations. This was the case in London in 1923, when he led a march campaigning for dominion status.[6]

Annie Besant submitted the bill to her politician friends in the labor movement.[7] It was passed on its first reading, and was then sent to the commission for presentation to the House of Lords. However, this never happened, as the labor movement lost the next elections.

At the start of 1922, Annie Besant announced that she had just appointed Jinarajadasa Vice President, stating that he was undoubtedly the best-known figure among the leaders, due to his international visits.

That year, he made his first grand tour of Europe. He visited Austria, Bulgaria, Romania, Czechoslovakia, Germany, Denmark, Norway, Sweden, and Finland, before returning to England, and traveling from there to Ireland and Wales. Under his leadership, a Muslim league was formed within the Theosophical Society. The aim was to develop the study of relationships between Islamic teaching and other traditions.

He arrived in Rio on October 10, 1928. He was well-received, especially due to his good Spanish and Portuguese. He visited Argentina, Bolivia, Peru, Costa Rica, Nicaragua, Honduras, El Salvador, Guatemala, Mexico, Cuba and finally Puerto Rico. It is worth noting that the Catholic Church was opposed to this tour. When he returned to this region in 1938–1939, it again attempted to bring about the failure of his conferences, even using its influence to get his entry visa for Peru refused.

On the international scene, most countries were suffering in the aftermath of the 1929 financial depression. In November, Jinarajadasa indicated that he did not want to be a candidate for President of the Theosophical Society, although many invited him to stand. Letters written during his visit to France show that his health remained fragile.

Jinarajadasa was elected head of the *Esoteric School*, taking over from Leadbeater in 1934. In June 1938, he was in London. During the war, the center of London became pivotal for support and aid to the European Continent. He also played a courageous civilian role as a *Fire Guard*,[8] a civil air raid protection volunteer.

On February 17, 1946, he took over as the new president of the Theosophical

---

[5] Services Tomorrow: Theosophical Society, Kensington Town hall, Mr C.Jninarajadasa, *Times*, November 22 1923.

[6] Arrangements for Today, Indian's March for Dominion Rule, *Times*, May 30 1923, Mr C. Jinarajadasa, Kensington Town hall, 8.

[7] Georges Fisher, "Un Trait d'Union : Annie Besant (1847–1933)," *Revue Tiers-Monde*, tome 15, no 58, (Paris, Armand Colin), 350.

[8] Fire Guard: *Air Raid Precautions.*

Society. There was much rebuilding to do. This became Jinarajadasa's main focus during his presidential mandate. He was also very committed to restoring order in the domain of Adyar. He faced a drop in membership and consequently in income from fees. In 1950, activities behind the Iron Curtain stopped. Russian branches and a Polish branch in exile were formed. In Spain, Theosophical activities were banned for 30 years under Franco. From 1950 to 1951, Jinarajadasa also worked continually to bring out a new edition of *Occult Chemistry*, with the addition of his many diagrams.

Jinarajadasa arrived at the American headquarters near Chicago, on June 9, 1953. He intended to remain there for some time and to give lectures, but severe heart attacks and problems associated with his diabetes prevented him from doing so. On June 15, after a medical examination, he was confined to his bed. He spent his final days in a room in the American Headquarters. He passed on peacefully to the Eternal Orient in the afternoon of June 18.

Jinarajadasa, Freemason

Jinarajadasa was initiated to International Mixed Freemasonry in the United States in 1908, to the Droit Humain Lodge in Cleveland, by the representative of the Supreme Council, Sister Alida De Leeuw.

Jinarajadasa and the Development of Mixed Masonry in South America.

In 1916, the Droit Humain created the Argentine Federation, but the troubled political history of this country, with its numerous dictatorships, made it difficult for the Droit Humain to develop. The Federation struggled to function, due to a lack of members.

In Brazil, the first Lodge was consecrated in 1919. A jurisdiction emerged in 1934. The implantation of Lodges in Mexico began in 1921. This takeoff allowed a Federation to be created in the same year.[9]

In 1919, a Lodge was founded in San José in Costa Rica by Brother José Basiléo Acuna Zeledon, who was initiated in France while working as a nurse in the French army during the First World War. He translated the Rite of York into Spanish, giving it Theosophical connotations. He would go on to open Droit Humain Lodges in El Salvador and Panama, then Colombia.[10]

In March 1929, the M∴I∴B∴ (Most Illustrious Brother) Jinarajadasa, a member of the British Oriental Federation, obtained authorization to consecrate several Master Masons from Costa Rica to the 18th Degree, thus enabling the creation of a Rose Croix Chapter in San José. The *Servicio N° 82* Chapter was founded on June 6, 1929.[11] In the same year, the M∴I∴B∴ Jinarajadasa conferred the 30th Degree to several members, allowing the foundation of an Areopagus in 1934.[12]

Also in 1929, the M∴I∴B∴ Jinarajadasa founded a blue Lodge in Lima, Peru.[13] Brother Cadenas, a dignitary of a male Obedience, helped to create a Lodge named *Igualdad N° 632*. Its Worhipful Master was Brother Riofrio. He was appointed provisional delegate for the Supreme Council for Lima, and was then promoted to the 18th Degree. Brother José Pacheco Ochoa replaced him as Worhipful

---

[9] Noëlle Charpentier de Coysevox, *La Franc-Maçonnerie Mixte et le Droit Humain* (EDIMAF/Editions Maçonniques de France, 1999), 69.

[10] Charpentier de Coysevox, *La Franc-Maçonnerie Mixte et le Droit Humain.*

[11] Marc Grosjean, *Le Droit Humain International* (Paris: Detrad, 2002), 206.

[12] Grosjean, *Le Droit Humain International*, 207.

[13] *Bulletin International du Droit Humain*, 45th year, No 1 (Jan–March 1939): 1.

Master. We can observe that this Lodge took a particular interest in astrology and magnetism. A new Lodge, *Hermès* N° 637 was formed on June 2, 1933 and was led by Brother Francisco Leo Lorenzo. This Lodge was installed on July 4, 1933.[14]

In Chile, following lectures given by Jinarajadasa, the Droit Humain created four Lodges between 1930 and 1934. This made the creation of the Chilean Federation possible in 1934.[15]

In 1938, the M∴I∴B∴ Jinarajadasa visited Costa Rica and observed that the Droit Humain members were actively engaged in developing the Order.

In 1939, a triangle was set up in Panama on request of the M∴I∴B∴ Coronado. Since the M∴I∴B∴ Jinarajadasa had to interrupt his travels in America for personal reasons, the M∴I∴B∴ José Acuna, a philosopher, well-known writer, and professor at the University of Costa Rica, replaced him. He subsequently created a Lodge in Bogotá, Colombia. Thanks to the M∴I∴B∴ Jinarajadasa, several members received the 32nd degree by communication and formed the Central American and Caribbean Consistory, which was officially consecrated on February 15, 1944.[16]

In 1939, the M∴I∴B∴ Jinarajadasa also founded a Lodge in Guatemala, in Tegucigalpa.

According to the M∴I∴B∴ Jinarajadasa, the Droit Humain in South America encountered problems developing, particularly because of the mentality of certain Masons who were hostile to women's emancipation. However, he thought that time worked in favor of mixed Masonry.[17]

As for the other Latin American Countries, in 1938 and 1939, he tried in vain to get into Venezuela so that he could meet members of mixed Masonry there. He was refused entry to the country by the government.[18]

The development of mixed Masonry in South America and Central America was largely the result of Brother Raja's activities. In this country, he organized a group of Lodges of different Degrees and gave public conferences on Freemasonry, which were warmly received.[19]

The Father of Mixed Masonry in Chile

At a special meeting in Chicago on June 25, 1949, celebrating the golden jubilee of the foundation of the International Supreme Council, the M∴I∴B∴ Jinarajadasa stated that he had introduced mixed Masonry into Chile around twenty years ago, and that this was why he was now considered the Father of mixed Masonry in this country. The Ill∴ Sister Angelica de Lopez, 32nd Degree, also indicated this in a report of the *Igualdad* Lodge N° 632 at the Orient of Santiago de Chile.

During the summer of 1929, Brother Jinarajadasa came to Chile. He was received by theosophists from Valparaiso and Santiago, as well as by eminent members of the Grand Lodge of Chile, including brothers present today, full of energy and enthusiasm, [...] With luminous speed, Brother Jinarajadasa put in place the project of founding a Lodge with the three Symbolic Degrees, thus laying the foundations of what is now known as the Chilean Federation of

---

[14] Grosjean, *Le Droit Humain International*, 211.

[15] Charpentier de Coysevox, *La Franc-Maçonnerie Mixte et le Droit Humain*, 69.

[16] *Bulletin International Le Droit Humain*, new series, 2nd quarter 1992: 21–23.

[17] Grosjean, *Le Droit Humain International*, 211.

[18] *Bulletin International du Droit Humain*, 45th year, No 1 (Jan–March 1939): 2.

[19] Edith F. Armour, "Mr Jinanrajadasa as a Mason," *The American Theosophist* (March 1943): 61.

International Mixed Masonry, the Droit Humain.[20]

During this visit, members of the Grand Lodge of Chile and a group of Theosophical Society members asked for his authorization to start a mixed Lodge and to approve the admission requests of thirteen candidates. The request was sent there and then to the General Secretariat of the Supreme Council in Paris. On February 23, 1929, Jinarajadasa received a cable authorizing this creation. He decided to call this new Lodge "*Egalité*" (Equality).

Two days later, the M∴I∴B∴ Jinarajadasa carried out the consecration ceremony for the Lodge, which became N° 632 in the Droit Humain registers. Jinarajadasa's visit to Chile attracted the attention of Brothers and Sisters studying the spiritual disciplines.The mixed Order grew fast. Ten years later, there were thirteen Lodges.

When I was formally received by all the Lodges together in 1939, I was struck by the number of young women present. I knew that many of them were school teachers."[21]

From this date, the Droit Humain would enter a decade of rather remarkable progress. There were numerous affiliations from the Grand Lodge of Chile, and many requests from profanes interested in this new perspective. Thus, in 1930, the "Horus" and "Pythagoras" Lodges were founded in Santiago, followed by the "Isis" Lodge in 1932, then the "Orion", "Minerva" and "Osiris" Lodges in 1933, and the "Hiram" Lodge in 1934.

In 1940, in recognition of his exceptional services to Mixed Freemasonry and to the wellbeing of Humanity, the International Mixed Supreme Council accorded Jinarajadasa the 33rd Degree: the highest Degree of the Ancient and Accepted Scottish Rite.[22]

The Rite of Memphis

After leaving India in April 1923, Jinarajadasa undertook a lecture tour in Italy. He already held the 30th Degree of the Ancient and Accepted Scottish Rite within mixed Masonry. He would also be admitted into the *Sovereign Sanctuary of Palermo*, led by Reginald Gambier Mac Bean since July 12, 1921, and he rose to 33°–95° Degree of the Rite. It is worth emphasizing that the Sovereign Sanctuary did not proselytize and that its members were carefully selected. Reginald Gambier Mac Bean was British consul in Palermo and a member of the Theosophical Society.

A few months prior to his formal installation as head of the Sovereign Sanctuary of Palermo, on March 28, 1921, the Supreme Council of International Mixed Masonry, the Droit Humain, gave Mac Bean the Degree of Grand Inspector General, 33rd Degree of the Ancient and Accepted Scottish Rite.[23]

In 1925, when the Rite of Memphis had several Lodges, the *Sovereign Sanctuary of Palermo* was forced into hibernation because of the political changes in Italy and in order to preempt Mussolini's action against Masonry.

---

[20] *The Morning Star*, Bulletin of the Oriental Federation of the Droit Humain, M.S 1947–1950, Vol no 4 (First Quarter 1949), 61.

[21] Curuppumullage Jinarajadasa, *Women in Freemasonry* (London: Theosophical Publishing House, 1944), 9–10.

[22] Edith F. Armour, "Mr Jinanrajadasa as a Mason," 61.

[23] Curuppumullage Jinarajadasa, "Rite of Memphis," *The Morning Star*, Vol IX, n° 4 (Oct 1943): 54.

The Initiatory Annals state that:

Italian Freemasonry is currently persecuted by Mussolini's government... In order to spare our Italian Brothers troubles and persecution, the Sovereign Grand Master of the Rite of Memphis in Italy has decided to temporarily put the Rite into hibernation....[24]

Masonry was a secret organization and this secrecy allowed Mussolini to highlight the idea of a conspiracy.[25] On January 12, 1925, he presented a bill to regulate the activities of secret societies.[26]

However, in order to *keep the traditions of the order alive*, Mac Bean delivered a charter dated August 22, 1925 to a number of Brothers living outside Italy, authorizing them to form a Sovereign Sanctuary at the time and place of their choice. The five chosen brothers were: C.W. Leadbeater, J.I. Wedgwood, G.S. Arundale, O. Kollerstrom and C. Jinarajadasa.[27]

In retirement, Brother Mac Bean became a member of several Lodges and Chapters of the Droit Humain, such as the Isis Mark Lodge and the Saint Alban Chapter in England. For a period, he remained at the Theosophical Headquarters in Adyar, where he became Theosophical Society treasurer. In April 1926, he joined the Rising Sun of India Lodge n° 107, and he joined Rose Croix Chapter Loyalty n° 4 in 1930.[28]

Jinarajadasa's Thinking

One of the actions required of the Initiate to the Eleusinian Mysteries was that they touch the sacred basket containing the toys of *Dionysus*: the die (representing Platonic solids), the spinning top, the model of the atom, the sphere, the earth and the mirror (a symbol of the seven planes on which the Logos is reflected).

Jinarajadasa's major contribution undoubtedly lies in his message emphasizing the *beauty of nature*. He believed that within nature was a mysterious law presiding over its construction. This law did not belong to the domains of chemistry or physics, but to Art. It was what he called the *law of radiance*. The essential attribute of Nature was its beauty, but this beauty expressed a geometrical conception. This was confirmed as science entered more deeply into the mysteries of Nature.[29] Today, certain mathematicians seek an aesthetic pleasure in their work or in mathematics in general. They see mathematics as an art or even a creative activity. Comparisons are often made with music and poetry. They suggest that there are deep links between mathematics, poetry and philosophy.[30]

In 1940, Godfrey Harold Hardy, a British mathematician, wrote that:

The mathematician's patterns, like the painter's or the poet's, must be beautiful; the ideas like the colors or the words, must fit together in a harmonious way.[31]

[24] *Initiatory Annals/Annales Initiatiques*, N° 22, July-September 1925, 273–274.
[25] Aldo A. Mola, *Storia delle Massoneria Italiana delle Origini ai Giorni Nostri* (Milan: Edizioni Tascabili Bompiani, 2013), 560–561.
[26] Fulvio Conti, *Storia della Massoneria Italiana dal Risorgimento al Fascismo*, (Bologna: Società Editrice Il Mulino, 2003) 314–315.
[27] Gregory Tillett, "The Esoteric within The Exoteric, Esoteric Schools within The Theosophical Movement" (paper presented to The Theosophical History Conference, San Diego, 1992), 23.
[28] Curuppumullage Jinarajadasa, "Rite of Memphis," *The Morning Star*, Vol IX, n° 4 (Oct 1943), 54.
[29] Curuppumullage Jinarajadasa, *L'Evolution Occulte de l'Humanité* (Paris: Publications Théosophiques, 1950), 226.
[30] Fabien Tarby, *La philosophie d'Alain Badiou* (Paris: L'Harmattan, 2005), 25.
[31] Godfrey Harold Hardy, *A Mathematician's Apology* (New York: Cambridge University Press, 1940), 85.

In a text entitled *"La beauté en mathématiques"* (Beauty in Mathematics) François Le Lionnais, a chemical engineer and mathematician with a love of literature observed that:

> *That is how beauty unfolds in mathematics as in the other sciences, as in the arts, as in life and in nature. Sometimes comparable to that of pure music, of great painting, or of poetry....*[32]

Jinarajadasa thought that:

> *We all believe in science. But our idea of a law of Nature is nothing like what the theologians claim are the divine laws. These are the commandments of an individual whose will is the law. But when we think scientifically, by "Law" we mean the fact that a certain cause will produce a given effect, without exception [...].*[33]

In 1959, David Bohm,[34] a physics theorist, discovered Krishnamurti's work, *First and Last Freedom*.[35] What interested him more specifically was the in-depth examination of the *observers and thing observed* question. This interrogation had long been at the heart of his own work, *Quantum Theory.*

In 1970, Fritjof Capra wrote *The Tao of Physics*. In this work, he established a parallel between quantum physics and certain teachings of eastern philosophies, and affirmed a pantheist vision of the universe.

Thus, Jinarajadasa proved to be particularly close to contemporary scientific speculations when he stated that his vision was not something to be accepted as a revelation, but a science that should be tested at every step of our exploration.[36]

---

[32] François Le Lionnais, ed., *Les Grands Courants de la Pensée Mathématique* (Paris: Librairie Scientifique et Technique A. Blanchard, 1962), 457–458.

[33] Curuppumullage Jinarajadasa, *L'Evolution Occulte de l'Humanité*, 203–204.

[34] David Bohm, "Ma rencontre avec Krishnamurti," *Revue Aurores* 18 (1981).

[35] Jiddu Krishnamurti, *First and Last Freedom* (London: V. Gollancz, 1954).

[36] Curuppumullage Jinarajadasa, *A New Conception of Theosophy* (Kessinger, 2010).

The Impact of European Freemasonry on the Turkish Civil Society

Emanuela Locci[1]

The will of the present paper is investigating on past and - somehow - present impact produced by the Masonic institution in Turkish civil society. To take in the issue a brief outline on Freemasonry origins is mandatory.

The speculative Freemasonry was founded in England in 1717 and its roots go back to the church and cathedral builders' guilds from the fifteenth until the seventeenth century that enriched major European cities with their works of engineering and construction. Since the end of the seventeenth century, however, the guilds had been going through a crisis due to the decrease of construction projects. Freemasonry had its direct origins from the craft guilds, and it took on new targets connected with the culture of the Enlightenment, characterizing itself as a cosmopolitan association. It was aimed at promoting the well-being of the individual and for society as a whole through ongoing education, regardless of differences in language, religion, nationality and political ideology.

In the same way as in the European countries, its expansion also affected the Mediterranean and the Near East, along with the colonial expansion. In fact, Freemasonry expanded in many countries outside Europe.

The appearance of the Masonic institution in the Ottoman Empire dates back to 1738[2] and in this context Freemasonry returned in a certain way to its origins because according to many scholars, its roots go deep into the Mediterranean civilization, along with that of ancient Egypt, the Jerusalem of Solomon, and Hellenic culture, even if this hypothesis is unproven due to the lack of clear documentation.

In order to fully understand the extent of cultural relations caused by the presence of Freemasonry in the Ottoman Empire, it is necessary to consider the situation of this vast state in the time span that goes from the entrance of the institution to the period of the height of its activities, which is identified as the beginning of the main attraction of the Institution for the Ottoman civil society[3].

The Empire was founded in about 1300, and it had gone through almost four hundred years of unscathed history, but in the first half of the eighteenth century it was going through a period of deep crisis. It was afflicted by military defeats, territorial concessions, especially in the European territories. Its supremacy was no longer absolute. Although it still remained a giant in terms of territory, it was affected by the evolution of the countries beyond its borders.[4] This is true not only from the technological point of view but also from a cultural and social one. While in the Empire

---

[1] Faculty of Political Science, University of Cagliari. Ph.D. in History, Institutions and International Relationship of Asia and Africa in Modern and Contemporary History, with a doctorate thesis entitled: "Il cammino di Hiram. La massoneria dall'Europa all'Impero Ottomano."
[2] See Thierry Zarcone, Mystiques, Philosophes et Franc-Maçons en Islam, (Paris, Maisonneuve, 1993) p. 189.
[3] See Halil Inalcik, Turkey and Europe in History, (Istanbul, Eren, 2006) pp. 50-51.
[4] See Erik Zurcher, Storia della Turchia. Dalla fine dell'impero ottomano ai giorni nostri, (Roma, Donzelli Editore, 2007), pp. 61-82.

doi: 10.18278/rscs.4.1.6

there was a decline of the arts mainly because of economic problems, Europe was treading new ground and going alone new roads, and the philosophical Enlightenment pervaded Europe.

The Enlightenment revolutionized the lives of an entire continent. The eighteenth century was for the Empire a century of a deep crisis as said before during which, however, the need for necessary reforms concerning the outdated economic and social state system had been understood. There was a need to discover the outside world in order to understand the reasons for the military success or economic dynamism, that dynamism which the Empire had now lacked for too long and that led to its system being obsolete.

During the reign, of Sultan Ahmed III[5] even a wider technological gap that the kingdom had accumulated towards the West could be noted. The Sultan sought to remediate this by trying to innovate the functioning of the institutions, but these attempts failed partly because of the pressure of powerful conservative groups. There was then a transition period which registered an even a stronger awareness of the real conditions of the Empire, and what was the actual power of the neighbouring countries. The latter continued to push the boundaries and economic trade extended its influence in Ottoman ports. The true and real reforms would only start in the nineteenth century when the European presence became more evident.

Freemasonry arrived early in areas which were far away from England,

reaching the Ottoman Empire nearly twenty years after its conversion from the operative Freemasonry into the speculative one[6]. During the first fifty years of its presence in the major imperial cities it was but one of the many manifestations of the European presence, which during those years was becoming more evident. It was also influential because of the always more unstable and decadent situation of the Empire. The contacts, and social and cultural relations between members of the Freemasonry, and the local people were in practice non-existent. The Ottomans did not tolerate Freemasonry, because for them it was a foreign association, composed of foreigners[7]. They were seen as the bearers of Western ideals, a modern culture that was badly amalgamated with the social structure, traditions, and above all even the religion of the majority of the Ottomans. In particular, the British Masons considered Freemasonry a "thing" of its own, which represented their national identity, and felt no need to integrate people who had a completely different cultural background from their own within the lodges.

We are therefore in the presence of a case of nationalist Freemasonry, in the sense of Freemasonry that was practiced by Europeans, the bearers of traditions and customs that remained confined to the European community[8].

The situation changed only later, thanks to the much more enlightened French Masons. They, unlike the British, believed in a universal Freemasonry, and had no conception of a national institution

---

[5] Sultan Ahmed III (1673 - 1736) ruled the Ottoman Empire from 1703 to 1730, his reign known as the "Tulip Age". His attempt willed to introduce some reforms in order to update the State apparatus. He encouraged philosophy and science education. His reforming action was hampered by the military corps of the Janissaries, beholding the reform projects as a threat to their status.

[6] See Thierry Zarcone, Mystiques, ….p. 187.

[7] That is strengthened by referencing Masonic lodges registers, demonstrating that - at the time of lodges establishment - the members were all European.

[8] Paul Dumont, Freemasonry in Turkey: a by-product of western penetration, *European Review* 13, n.3, (2005), p. 482.

and soon embarked on the policy of Masonic propaganda. This consisted of the constant spread of Masonic ideals[9]. This was also done above all outside of the community which was always quite small and was not able to provide an adequate number of followers. The only way forward was to involve other communities. First of all, they tried to introduce prominent people from other foreign communities, Italians, Greeks, Armenians and Jews into the French lodges.

It was in the late sixties and mid-seventies of the nineteenth century when the greatest opening of the French Freemasonry towards the Ottoman society was observed. It was thanks to the work of Louis Amiable[10], a lawyer who was the head of the French Freemasonry in Istanbul. Due to his incessant work, several lodges were founded in the area made up of people of different social status, culture and religion. He made Masonic Western culture accessible to the Ottomans by doing a very simple thing, that is translating the rituals and lectures that were carried out in the lodge into the Ottoman language. This step bridged the gap between West and East, and created a system of mutual understanding, which demonstrated what had already been said by the Emir Abdel Kader[11] who was a mason, that there was no distance between Masonic and Islamic philosophy[12].

The events described above were the first attempts of socio-cultural inclusion. Freemasonry then became the bearer of the values connected to the Enlightenment - the cultural, social and philosophical current that began in England around the eighteenth century but reached its maximum development in France. The term "Enlightenment" means generally any form of ideas that want to "light up" the mind of men, unenlightened by ignorance and superstition, by using the critique of reason and the contribution of science but also of the classics. All of this is found in Masonic philosophy, which is the same that at first influenced European Masons and later the Ottoman affiliates. The Masons learnt Masonic culture by studying the Greek classics, from Pericles to Hippocrates, studying and deepening their reflections. They focused on the concept of democracy, which was alien to the Ottoman political system. The encounter with Western culture affected many areas, not least music. In fact even today, one of the most popular composers in Turkey is Amadeus Mozart who played a major role in the Masonic tradition[13].

It is difficult to indicate what the contribution of Freemasonry was in terms of culture in a society which is completely different from the European

[9] Louis Amiable, De la situation maçonique a Costantinople, en Grece et en Italie, (Aix en provence, Remondet-Aurin, 1895), p. 5.
[10] Louis Amiable was born in Montbrison on February 16, 1837. He was educated in law in Paris and in 1861 he achieved a PhD in jurisprudence. In 1864-1870 he had been living in Constantinople, where he reformed the attorneys' fellowship of the capital. After this experience, he returned home for about twenty years and again at Constantinople in 1889. A number of his works related to divorce and legal separation of powers between Church and State. He died in January 25, 1897 in Aix en Provence.
[11] The Emir Abdel Kader (1808-1883) was born into a deeply religious family, he traveled widely in his youth and when back to Algeria in 1830 - just before the arrival of the French corps - he began a military career that saw him as mastermind in a plenty of anti-French riots. Finally defeated in 1844, he was exiled to France and released only in 1852 to go to Damascus. It is considered the 'Father of the Homeland' by the Algerians; by French people seen as a native illuminated. For further details see, Bruno Etienne, *Abdelkader*, (Paris, Hachette,1994).
[12] See Xavier Yacono, Abdel Kader franc-maçon, in *Humanisme* 57, (1966), p. 17.
[13] For further insights on Mozart and links with the Masons, please refer to Eugenio Lazzari, L' ideologia massonica nella vita e nella musica di Mozart, (Foggia, Bastogi, 2007).

one, and it is a subject that has hardly been studied compared to the central theme of Freemasonry. It is possible to advance the hypothesis, however, supported by reliable sources which indicate that thanks to the French Masons, with their openness and Enlightenment tradition, there was a first real contact between Western culture and the Ottomans.

This was represented by the Masonic institution and Eastern culture, imbued with religious ideals. Ottoman Masons, so tied to the Muslim religion, had approached the masonry only after establishing with full conviction that Freemasonry and Islam were not in conflict.

During the second half of the nineteenth century Ottoman literature was influenced by European literature, for example such intellectuals as Namik Kemal[14] and Tevfik Fikret[15] who, despite the despotism of Sultan Abdülhamid II[16] and Abdulaziz[17], did not stop exalting and writing about purely European ideals and concepts such as liberty, equality, homeland and nation. The relationship between Freemasonry and the Ottoman civil society can be seen from two perspectives: one is the encounter between a society that had already gained its internal experience of fraternity, through the Sufi brotherhoods, which for years had represented the centre of social life. They represented the most

important example of Ottoman sociality. Based on the study of the characteristics of the brotherhoods it is evident that they had things in common with the Masons, such as liberalism, non-conformism and to some extent anti-clericalism. Through mutual knowledge Masonic rituals were welcomed in one of the most important brotherhoods in the panorama of Ottoman sufi, the Bektāshiyyah[18], that in fact made some Masonic rituals their own. The other aspect is that of opposition, which sees the Masons as the bearers of purely European values and ideals, which were not accepted by the Ottoman civil society.

In conclusion it is possible to affirm that Freemasonry constituted for Turkey a vector of modern ideals since between the nineteenth and twentieth centuries, it accompanied the introduction of the ideas of progress and liberalism[19].

In the lodges there was also the meeting of men of different ethnicities, who were working in harmony inside the temple, and who cohabited outside but rarely had social relations, as all the ethnicities were isolated from a social perspective.

The lodges were spaces for discussion and the exchange of ideas. Here there were discussions on Masonic issues but also on issues related to the advancement of science or other subjects that had affected public opinion.

---

[14] Namik Kemal (1840-1888) was a poet, writer, reformer who influenced the Ottoman Young Turk movement. He tried to reconcile the principles of the French Revolution with the Muslim tradition.

[15] Tevfik Fikret (1867-1915) poet, is deemed the Father of the modern school of Turkish poetry .

[16] Abdülhamid II (1842-1918), the second son of Sultan Abdülmecit, was the 34th Ottoman sultan and ruled from 1876 to 1909 by an absolute monarch. After the Constitutional Revolution of 1908 lasted on the throne for nine months, but deposed after the failure of the counterrevolution of 1909. Along with his family, was exiled in Thessaloniki but in 1912, when the city turned Greek, the former Sultan was moved back in Istanbul, where he spent the last years. He died February 10, 1918 - a few months before the defeat in WWI and the resulting dissolution of the Empire.

[17] Abdulaziz, son of Mahmud II, was Sultan in 1861-1876.

[18] The Sufi brotherhood Bektāshiyyah was founded in the early Sixteenth century, about two hundred years after the death of its ideologist, Haci Bektaş, who envisioned it as a-syncretic doctrine whilst the structural organization was a posthumous step.

[19] Angelo Iacovella, Il triangolo e la mezzaluna, (Istanbul, IICI, 1997), p. 46.

Finally I would like to say a few words about the situation at present. There are no sociological studies about how the people consider the Institution. However, it is possible to observe that the situation of Freemasonry in Turkey is quite good.

This can be seen from the presence of different Obediences: besides the National Grand Lodge[20] which represents traditional free Masonry there are also present other Grand Lodges which work under the supervision of other Obediences. Among these there is the Liberal Grand Lodge[21] and also the Female Grand Lodge of Turkey[22] which is made up of about 2300 women. The women's obedience is composed of about 20 lodges which can be found in the most important cities of Turkey.

The numerical strength of the various allegiances grows year by year - through the foundation of new lodges - even in smaller urban centers, such as the sense of growing closeness to the institution of civil society. The existence of a female obedience - which has been operating for nearly twenty five years - clarifies the closeness of women; although it's just still the elite approaching the Masonry, however, is a promising sign of a potential development in Masonic experience .

So the Turkish Freemasonry, also thanks to the work begun by Sahir Akev Talat[23] in early 2000 and then pursued by other Grand Master occurring to the office - notably by Remzi Sanver[24], able to encouraged even more relations between the Institution and folks, through the use of socials - is succeeding in dissemination and esteem of Masonry out of the line of its very epoch.

---

[20] The National Grand Lodge of Turkey stems from the Ottoman Grand Orient, founded in 1909. Today it's the most important allegiance of Turkey, with some 15,000 swearers scattered both in major cities and small communities.

[21] This obedience is the outcome of the schism occurred in 1965 within the National Grand Lodge of Turkey. The first Grand Master of Irregular Obedience in 1966-1969 was Orhan Hançerlioğlu.
CELIL, Layiktez, Türkiye'de masonluk tarihi, 1957-1970, (Istanbul, Yenılık Basimevi, 2001), pp. 167-187.

[22] La Female Grand Lodge of Turkey was established in 1991. It is part of CLIMAF, an institution that brings together eight European women's obedience.

[23] Akev Talat Sahir was born in Istanbul in 1925, admitted as Freemason in 1953, became Grand Master in 1998, ushering in an era of openness of Masonic Institution towards civil society.

[24] Remzi Sanver was born in Istanbul in 1971 - as a youngster initiated to the Freemasons, following his father footsteps - became Grand Master in May 2009; two years later, in 2011, he was reappointed. In 2013 a brand new election tournament took place, which Remzi Sanver could not apply to since the protocol of the Grand Lodge prohibits two terms in a row.

www.ingramcontent.com/pod-product-compliance
Lightning Source LLC
Chambersburg PA
CBHW081651270326
41933CB00018B/3432